"I am delighted to offer words of endorsement for Michael Timmis' inspiring autobiography. I am proud to call him a friend and truly admire his extraordinary journey of faith described herein.

"Having been raised in a traditional Roman Catholic family in Detroit during the 1950's, after his mother's death during his adolescence, Michael's heart hardened. Although he continued to be a practicing Catholic, his relationship with God remained very formal. As he and his wife, Nancy, raised their two children, Michael and Laura, he became a successful entrepreneur, lawyer, and investor. But all the while, he was empty inside.

"Then at forty-three years old, one November night his wife literally forced him to a meeting of evangelical Christians at their local country club. Something stirred in his heart. Shortly after that evangelical awakening and coming to know the Lord Jesus, Michael and his wife began inviting others to share their faith journey, reflecting on the Scriptures. "FIRE" was born: Faith, Intercession, Repentance, Evangelism.

"As Michael faced times of doubt and frustration in his role as a father, he came to understand prayer to the Lord as his only solution: His relationship with his son changed, and now his son shares in his missionary spirit and commitment to share the good news of Jesus Christ. Well known among Promise Keepers and for his leadership of International Prison Fellowship, the journey of Michael Timmis has truly been a journey of the heart. He has met almost every major world figure during his travels around the world and, clearly, the one most important person of all—Jesus Christ.

"It is an engaging and also challenging autobiography. Highly recommended!"

—CARDINAL ADAM MAIDA, Archbishop of Detroit

"I have known Mike Timmis as a man who 'walks the talk,' a successful businessman who devotes his life to the underprivileged: inner-city schoolchildren and international prison ministry. However, only in this book have I learned the trials and triumphs that formed his life and faith."

— PHILIP YANCEY, author of more than twenty books, including *Prayer: Does It Make Any Difference?* and *What's So Amazing About Grace?*

"The life of Mike Timmis is a powerful testimony to what can happen when evangelicals and Catholics work together as brothers and sisters in Christ. His story demonstrates that we are more fully and faithfully Catholic as we rejoice in the fellowship of all who confess Jesus Christ as Lord."

— FR. RICHARD JOHN NEUHAUS, editor-in-chief; *First Things*

Between Two Worlds

The Spiritual Journey of an Evangelical Catholic

Mike Timmis

WITH HAROLD FICKETT

NAVPRESS®

OUR GUARANTEE TO YOU

For a free catalog
of NavPress books & Bible studies call
1-800-366-7788 (USA) or 1-800-839-4769 (Canada).

www.navpress.com

The Navigators is an international Christian organization. Our mission is to advance the gospel of Jesus and His kingdom into the nations through spiritual generations of laborers living and discipling among the lost. We see a vital movement of the gospel, fueled by prevailing prayer, flowing freely through relational networks and out into the nations where workers for the kingdom are next door to everywhere.

NavPress is the publishing ministry of The Navigators. The mission of NavPress is to reach, disciple, and equip people to know Christ and make Him known by publishing life-related materials that are biblically rooted and culturally relevant. Our vision is to stimulate spiritual transformation through every product we publish.

© 2008 by Mike Timmis

ISBN-13: 978-1-60006-248-3
ISBN-10: 1-60006-248-2

Cover design by The DesignWorks Group, David Uttley, www.thedesignworksgroup.com
Creative Team: Caleb Seeling, Keith Wall, Darla Hightower, Amy Spencer, Arvid Wallen, Kathy Guist

Some of the anecdotal illustrations in this book are true to life and are included with the permission of the persons involved. All other illustrations are composites of real situations, and any resemblance to people living or dead is coincidental.

Unless otherwise identified, all Scripture quotations in this publication are taken from the *New American Bible*. Copyright © 2002 by United States Conference of Catholic Bishops. Other versions used include HOLY BIBLE: NEW INTERNATIONAL VERSION® (NIV®). Copyright © 1973, 1978, 1984 by International Bible Society. Used by permission of Zondervan Publishing House. All rights reserved; and the *King James Version* (KJV).

Library of Congress Cataloging-in-Publication Data

Timmis, Mike.
  Between Two Worlds : the spiritual journey of an evangelical catholic / Mike Timmis with Harold Fickett.
    p. cm.
  ISBN 978-1-60006-248-3
  1. Evangelicalism--Relations--Catholic Church. 2. Catholic Church--Relations--Evangelicalism. I. Fickett, Harold. II. Title.
BR1641.C37T56 2008
280'.042--dc22

                    2007044506

Printed in the United States of America

1 2 3 4 5 6 7 8 / 12 11 10 09 08

To my beloved wife, Nancy; our daughter, Laura;
our son, Michael; our daughter-in-law, Laura; and
our grandchildren, Bailey, Teresa, Josie, and Michael III

Contents

Foreword

You are about to read a truly inspiring and moving story. It will move you because my friend Mike Timmis opens himself, not just to his successes but to the heartaches few people could know or would want to know in their own lives. But Mike's story will inspire you because God has redeemed his and his family's suffering and used them in remarkable ways to touch others.

You'll be inspired as well because this is the story of a poor kid from the working-class streets of Detroit who went on to become an outstanding lawyer, businessman, and evangelist, bringing the gospel to millions around the world. The lesson of Mike's book is one we can never tire of hearing: that God takes the weak, broken, and poor and turns them into mighty instruments of His grace.

Over the last nearly twenty years, I have come to know Mike as one of my very closest friends and colleagues. I therefore can tell you that the story you're about to read is about the real thing. Mike is a man of unique talent and deep devotion.

It would be hard to find two people closer than Mike and me. One reason is we're a lot alike. Similar backgrounds. Fighters. Ambitious and determined, sometimes to the extent of being called stubborn. And now we share the same vision for the world.

(We have much in common, except Mike never went to prison. I tell him there's always time. As it turns out, that is where he spends much of his time.)

But there is more to this book than just one man's conversion. Mike and I hope through our lives to remind believers that there is one Lord, one faith, one baptism — that all true Christians coming from whatever their confessions can join together and affirm the essentials of the Christian faith entrusted to the saints once for all.

The Christian faith today is locked in a life-and-death struggle, assaulted by radical Islam on one side and anti-theistic secularism on the other. Christians, of course, have always been persecuted, often giving their lives to protect the faith. But today's conflict is unique. Radical Islamo-fascists, basing their ideology on a combination of Nazi teachings and the most literal reading of the Qur'an, seek to do nothing less than destroy the Christian west and eliminate Christians and Jews from the face of the earth. It is impossible to overestimate the threat. I've read their literature. I've studied the influences on their writers. And what we're seeing is the assault of evil in the most threatening manner. Western culture has not yet awakened to the seriousness of the threat.

At the same time, our culture, which was created by Christianity, is rebelling against the very source of its authority and origin. The likes of Richard Dawkins, the Oxford evolutionary biologist, Christopher Hitchens, the British social critic, Daniel Dennett, and Sam Harris have recently sold millions of books that aggressively promote atheism. They are a new genre; Hitchens calls himself an "anti-theist." These advocators want to ban the teaching of religion to our children and, ironically not unlike radical Islamo-fascists, purge Christian influence from society.

The point to remember is that such attacks are not because we are from the Reformed tradition or Baptist or Catholic or Orthodox. We are under assault because we are followers of Jesus Christ. If we don't find a way to stand together and right the great scandal of our faith, which is no longer the Cross but rather our divisions, we will be easy prey for one group or the other — for both.

Nearly twenty years ago I began meeting for informal discussions with a group of evangelical and Catholic scholars led by Richard John Neuhaus. We'd been drawn together by what the great Baptist theologian Timothy George calls "ecumenism of the trenches," our common labors.

Over the years this group discovered that while there are many differences in our confessions and traditions (which are not to be minimized), there is much more that we hold in common — the great tenets of the Christian faith. We issued some important papers, including one in the critical area that caused the Reformation called "Gift of Salvation," in which we reaffirmed our common belief in justification by faith alone, specifically what the Reformers called *sola fide*. On the Protestant side, we've also come to understand that our belief in Scripture alone does not undermine the importance of tradition. We have been learning from one another. We have confirmed the great positions taken in the creeds and learned what it is to call one another and treat one another as brothers and sisters in Christ.

For me this has become a passion, first because of the biblical injunction in John 17 where Jesus prays, "Father, may they be one with one another as I am one with You, so the world will know that You did send me." As Francis Schaeffer prophetically warned, if we do not seek unity, the world has the right to judge whether we are true Christians. So there is a compelling biblical mandate that we seek unity wherever possible—not a wishy-washy ecumenism where we reduce things to the lowest common denominator but a vigorous assertion of what we can share in service of the truth.

As you'll read in the pages that follow, it was because of my passion for this effort that Mike Timmis in 1991 joined me in the ministry of Prison Fellowship. Mike had never had any interest in prisons, but having been converted to a lively evangelical faith as a Roman Catholic, he was the man God called to stand with me—two brothers together, evangelizing, defending the faith, and witnessing—that we would reach across the great confessional divides together in Christ as we carried on the incredible ministry of Prison Fellowship.

Neither of us has abandoned our confessing traditions. I'm a Baptist and Mike is Catholic, and if anything we've both been strengthened in our own convictions. Yet we have learned from each other. Mike has certainly learned how to be a soul winner. He's one of the most winsome evangelists I know. I've seen his passion for bringing others to a personal relationship with Christ, both within and outside of the Catholic Church. And I have learned from Mike's commitment to the poor and his devotional life. We live near one another in Florida, so we frequently take long walks together. Mike is a multitasker, as I am, so a walk consists of pushing as hard as we can for two miles until we're gasping for breath, all the while sharing Scriptures or praying. Mike has convicted me about the need to pray continuously.

But I hope I'm a little more prudent about it than he is. Once he was peddling his bike as hard as he could through a residential area, head down, praying fervently, when he suddenly met the front of an automobile pulling out of a driveway. The bike stopped abruptly, but Mike didn't. He ended up sprawled in the grass on the other side of the driveway. The poor driver, an elderly gentleman, thought he had just killed a bicycle rider. But Mike got up, brushed the dirt off, and walked home. (The bike had had its last ride.)

Now you'd think that someone would learn from such an experience. But Mike, as you'll discover in this book, is a hard-headed Irishman. On a later occasion he was doing exactly the same thing, bicycling furiously and praying intensely, and this time he hit the back of a parked SUV. The bike crumpled and Mike flew straight ahead, crashing through the back window and landing in the vehicle's back seat. Fortunately the driver was not in the car (he might have been killed), but he *was* watching from the curb, wide-eyed. Mike sustained a few bruises, and again he had to walk home. This time it cost him $1,800 to repair the SUV. So while I try to follow Mike's example of continuous prayer, I do try to watch where I'm going.

As much as anything, these little episodes give you a hint about the character of Mike Timmis. He's not the kind of guy who sits around in committee meetings. He sees a problem and moves straight ahead to fix it—which is why, coupled with his great mind and loving heart, he has been so successful.

Mike succeeded me as chairman of Prison Fellowship International ten years ago. He was the perfect person to take the reins because he had traveled all over the world, had an evangelist's heart, and was sympathetic to people of all confessions. When he became chairman PFI ministered in sixty countries. Today PFI has outreaches in 114 countries.

As you read this warm and stirring story, I hope you'll take away two critical lessons. The first is that we must reach into the prisons of America and the world. As a theologian told me when I started the ministry of Prison Fellowship in 1976, it is wonderful to be doing something in which you know you are in the will of God. What he meant was that there is a specific mandate in Scripture to care for prisoners, and when these men and women are converted, they make the most glorious witnesses. This is truly doing the gospel and making the invisible kingdom visible.

The second lesson is the need for all true Christians to rally around what C. S. Lewis called "mere Christianity"—the non-negotiable fundamentals of the Christian faith entrusted to the saints (see Jude 3) and held in common by all Christians. All Christians are called not only to practice their faith in their own confessing traditions, but also to reach out across the confessions and take true Christians by the hand, standing rejoicing as brothers and sisters together in obedience to God's call.

—Chuck Colson

A Word Before

Catholics still speak at times of evangelicalism as another religion, while evangelicals often suspect that Catholics are saved, if at all, *despite* their church and not *because* of it. I am a cradle Catholic, a committed Christian, and the chairman of a global ministry that works across the denominations. I've experienced both sides of the confessional divide as few others have, and my story and the lessons I've learned may help those who want to set aside disagreements, change antagonistic attitudes, and find common ground—as well as those who simply want to better understand the brother who converted to Catholicism or the formerly Catholic cousins who now worship in an evangelical megachurch.

We know about the differences, but what underlying unity accounts for these transitions? How can we discover and embrace this unity, particularly as we attempt to show Christ's love to a broken world? That has been a major theme woven throughout my life, and that is the spirit in which I write.

—MIKE TIMMIS

Chapter One

Taking Life into My
Own Hands

On January 18, 1991, I was flying in a small two-engine plane in east-central Africa from Burundi to Kenya. Our party had just come from a wonderful meeting with Burundi's President Pierre Buyoya where we'd shared the gospel with him and a number of cabinet ministers. Still, we were somewhat anxious because the Persian Gulf War had started the previous day. Right then, American fighters were in the air against Iraqi positions.

My wife, Nancy, and my son, Michael Jr., were with me, as well as Gene Dewey, the former second-in-command at the United Nations High Commissioner for Refugees, and Sam Owen, a fellow believer then living in Nairobi. This trip was part of the quiet diplomacy I had undertaken as a member of a group called The Fellowship. We worked on behalf of the poor by raising up Jesus with world leaders, one means of pursuing the ministry of reconciliation that Christ entrusted to His followers.

As we flew over northern Tanzania, the pilot was suddenly issued an order that we were to land immediately. I was sitting close enough to the cockpit to hear the squawking instructions coming over the radio. I quickly assured the pilot that we had the requisite permission to fly over Tanzanian air space. The State Department had issued an order to American citizens to stay

17

clear of Tanzania, an Iraq ally, so I made sure—or thought I had—that we had permission to fly over Tanzania en route to Kenya. The pilot relayed my protest to the Tanzanians.

"No, you do not have permission!" came the reply. "You must land immediately, or we will force you down."

We landed at the small city airport of Mwanza. As we stepped down onto the tarmac, a military jeep pulled up. A cadre of officials and police officers met us and immediately arrested the pilot and impounded the plane.

Their leader also demanded our passports. I was reluctant to give these up, because no matter what alternative flight arrangements we might be able to make, we would be stranded without passports. Because I had requested—and been granted—permission to fly over Tanzania, our detention was making me angry. (Later I found out that the flight service we were using had previously flouted Tanzanian regulations and had again on this occasion.) Because my family was with me, I restrained my temper. My jaw clenched, I reluctantly handed over my passport.

We were allowed to find our own accommodations in Mwanza, and we found a car that took us to the New Hotel Mwanza. I would hate to have seen the *old* Hotel Mwanza. We were the hotel's only guests, and for good reason. The first thing I did was check under the bed for bugs and rats.

As we caught our breath in our hotel room, I asked Nancy if she was afraid. "No, I'm not afraid," she said. "You are with me, our son is with us, and God is with us."

Even though we were stranded in an African backwater, I felt the same. I knew I was where God wanted us to be and felt—as I always have in my travels to what are now 114 nations—that God was going before me. In my many years of traveling on various missions, I've always felt protected by the special anointing that comes with God's commission. Lost geographically, I was still at home spiritually, and for that reason at peace.

Our party of five met for dinner in the hotel's restaurant. My family is Catholic, and Gene Dewey and Sam Owen were evangelicals, but the unity we knew in the Lord sustained us, even when the dinner turned out to be rancid.

After a little while, the hotel manager, having no other guests, joined us at our table. This made way for the night's entertainment. Four strapping young men in red overalls—the kind gas station attendants used to wear—came out, and with lamplight smiles launched into song:

My baaaaah-dy lies over the ocean,
My baaaaah-dy lies over the sea. . . .

Yes, they said "body" not "bonnie," and since we all felt an ocean away from home, the song struck us as hilarious. Then the quartet followed with "Home on the Range," and we nearly wept from laughing. We clapped and cheered, showing our appreciation to the young men. They had done us more good than they could possibly have known.

I spent the next day searching for transportation out of Mwanza. The others paid special attention to BBC radio reports on the progress of the war.

Within thirty-six hours, a plane flew in for us from Nairobi. We went out to the airport to meet it, eager to hightail it out of there. But when we arrived at the airport, no one seemed inclined to return our passports. Thankfully, Gene Dewey was already anticipating this. Because of his time with the United Nations, Gene had the most experience in dealing with government officials. He had also been a colonel in Vietnam and had a knack for being cool and fiercely determined at the same time. I kept asking him when he thought we'd get our passports back—and how. "Mike, don't worry about it," he'd say.

As we were walking out to the plane, bags in hand, with a couple of Tanzanian officials to the rear in escort, I looked over at Gene and said as forcefully as I could under my breath, "Gene, our passports!"

"Not now, Mike," he replied quietly but just as forcefully. "Just don't worry about it. Keep walking."

It wasn't until we were in the air that Gene unbuttoned his shirt and fished out all our passports.

"How did you get those?" I asked.

"I came out to the airport last night," he said. "I broke into the office and took them. If you had kept talking, they might have found out!"

Gene's street smarts reminded me of how I'd grown up and made my way. I asked myself, "How did I get here? How did a Catholic kid from the rough and gritty streets of Detroit end up on a trip meeting with presidents and prime ministers on behalf of Jesus?"

I've had many amazing, frightening, and heart-rending experiences as I've traveled the world in service to the King of kings. And one thing I can say for certain: When you entrust yourself completely to God and make yourself available to Him, you're in for an adventure.

☐ ☐ ☐

"Mike, the only way you can be ensured of success," my father once told me, "is if you take it into your own hands and go into the professions." I was an Irish Catholic kid from the battling

West Side of Detroit, the youngest of five children, keen on finding my own place in the world.

My father remains the strongest man I think I've ever known, with enormous hands, a powerful physique, and an energy that stayed with him into his nineties. I saw him lift a car out of a ditch when he was in his sixties, although he did injure his back. As young men, he and his brother Brian went out to western Canada, where they took jobs as real-live cowboys, breaking horses. Brian stayed, became a Mountie in Regina, Saskatchewan, and played professional football there. My dad returned to Ottawa and played wingback for the Ottawa Roughriders.[1] There he met an Irish girl who was both passionate and practical, and he had the good sense to ask for her hand.

My parents emigrated from Canada to Detroit in 1930, at the beginning of the Great Depression. My mother's uncle had moved there earlier from Ottawa and convinced my parents that the Motor City was one of the last places in North America where a man could find regular employment. Our relatives soon moved back to Ottawa, but my father and mother stayed, and Dad hired on with the city as a bus driver. He eventually worked his way up through the civil service system and retired as a bus station manager.

Most of his working life turned out to be far different from the spirited and reckless days as a cowboy and pro football player. I was the last of five children, separated in age by twelve years from my eldest sibling, Margaret Claire. My parents were well into their forties when I was born in 1939, and so I never knew my father as a young man. Or a particularly happy man—not at least until much later in his life when, in retirement, he was able to live on a farm and keep horses.

While I was growing up, I remember my dad collapsing into

his chair at the end of his long days. He'd take up one of Luke Short's westerns — he probably read every novel the man had ever written ten times. I can't say for certain whether he ever graduated from high school. I know he served in the Canadian forces in World War I, beginning in 1914 at seventeen. And since he was born in 1897, he might have left for the war before graduating.

We were a serious family, always working or studying or going to St. Brigid's, our local Catholic parish. Our faith was a great comfort to both my father and mother, but it was also a cause of concern as to the children's futures. My father felt that Irish Catholics were discriminated against, so he insisted that my brothers and I become doctors.

At the time, all of Detroit was divided into ethnic neighborhoods of Poles, Eastern European Jews, Irish, Germans, Italians, and so on. We lived in an Irish Catholic enclave. The houses stood one against the other on forty-foot lots, with bay windows to one side of half porches. The weave of that community was very close-knit. As a ten-year-old, I once cursed on a playground a block from home and received a slap for it when I came in ten minutes later for supper. A neighbor had heard what I said and promptly telephoned my mother.

But such strictures helped keep the city a safe and open place where I was free to roam. Not only did we not lock our front door, but I don't remember there being a key. From the age of eight or nine, I could walk down to the local candy store and then hop buses down to Woodward Avenue, where Hudson's, the giant department store, mounted huge Christmas window displays.

At the same time, the neighborhood had its own pugnacious code: You stood up to a fight or you simply couldn't live there. Taking a beating was far better than being constantly harassed, so I did a lot of fighting as a kid. I can remember coming home from school one winter day. My sister had taken the bus home from college, and one of the neighborhood bullies, whom I'll call Larry, had thrown an "ice ball" that hit her in the face.

My dad said to me, "Take care of him."

Larry's reputation as a bully was well earned, and I said, "Dad, this guy is going to kill me!"

"I don't care," Dad replied sternly. "You go out and you take care of him — now!"

Anger with my father for ordering this confrontation drove me out into the streets. When I caught sight of Larry, I ran after him, yelling at him vehemently. He hardly knew what hit him! I was so angry with Dad that I beat the living daylights out of the kid. I had him down on his back by the curb, where water was running from the snowmelt, and I whaled on him.

My father may have been so concerned about prejudice against Catholics because he'd had to overcome that obstacle when he started courting my mother. My dad's family was high-church Anglican. He converted when he married my mother, which wasn't much of a stretch, since high-church Anglicans worship in a liturgical style as close to Catholicism as Protestantism gets. Still, crossing to Rome was always an issue, especially at a time when Help Wanted signs included the postscript "No Irish Need Apply."

My mother's family, the O'Reillys, originally from County Clare, were Irish Catholics to the core. My mother was a petite woman, not more than five feet tall. In appearance, she was what they call dark Irish, with mahogany and cherry wood strands in her hair and a flame in her light-blue eyes. The O'Reillys, who owned brickyards, were far more well-to-do than my dad's family.

The pictures of my mother that I keep close by are candid shots; they show her as a young woman with the new bob of short hair that came in with the 1920s, striking a jaunty attitude. I can imagine this young Irish lass losing her head over my powerful, handsome father.

She was told never to have children because of a weak heart, and then she went and had five. Better educated than my dad, she had been to what was called a "normal school," or teacher's college. I would guess that many of our family's intellectual and creative gifts came through my mother. My brother Gerry, who the family called Sonny, would go on to be a famous cardiologist; Hilary, an outstanding surgeon; and both my sisters, Margaret Claire and Agnes Cecile, went to college and had marriages and careers that took them well up the economic ladder.

Once married, my mother never worked outside the home but gave herself completely and utterly to her husband and children. That didn't keep her from having a sharp tongue, or so my sisters claim; I never was cut deeply enough to remember her that way. It was not so much that I was the "baby" of the family, but that my mother's health was in serious decline by the time I reached early adolescence. She was too exhausted to protest against much of anything by then.

Both my father and my mother led our family in practicing our Catholic faith. In fact, when I think of my religious formation, I remember the faith as a distinctly family affair. Our devotions as a family made a great impression on me. We devoted the month of May to praying *with* Mary — not *to* Mary — to her Son, Jesus.

Every Sunday night, my whole family knelt down at seven o'clock and prayed for the conversion of Russia. My brothers Sonny and Hilary began to protest against the practice when they became busy medical students, but even then my parents insisted that the time be set aside.

On Tuesday evenings, we went to St. Brigid's for devotions, praying the rosary, making novenas, or listening as a "mission" was preached—what evangelical Protestants know as a revival service. These devotions largely disappeared from the Catholic Church after Vatican II in the early sixties and only now are being reinstated. The piety they encouraged came to be regarded as old-fashioned. Through these devotions, the Catholics of my parents' generation—and generations before them—experienced the Catholic faith as intensely personal. The devotions also encouraged them to recognize their faith as God's work in their lives. I experienced enough of this to understand clearly that my salvation was dependent on the completed work of Christ—not on my own righteousness. There was never a time when I was under the misimpression that my "works" would get me into heaven.

I attended the local parish school, St. Brigid's, where I was prepared for First Communion and Confirmation by the sisters who taught us. My first confession at the age of six saw me truly penitent, if confused. There were no secrets in our Irish Catholic family, and everyone wanted to know to what I had confessed. I told my brothers and sisters that I had admitted to adultery about a hundred times.

"You did?" they asked. "What did you mean?"

"That I picked my nose!"

I'm sure the priest about fell off the chair as he smothered his laughter.

Still, my First Communion was a memorable experience at which I received a child's prayer book—one that I only recently parted with when I gave it to my granddaughter on the occasion of her First Communion. It meant that much to me. Even as a young child, I took the privilege of being invited into communion with God very seriously. I think most children do, because they understand intuitively what it means to be God's child.

At St. Brigid's, we were schooled in the Baltimore Catechism, so when I was confirmed in the Catholic faith in fifth grade, I knew all the right answers to the classic questions: Who made us? Who is God? Why did God make us? In retrospect, I wish I had understood and experienced these rites of passage more in terms of an evolving relationship with Christ rather than as childhood milestones. Confirmation comes later now, when a child is about twelve or thirteen, which I think is good; older children are better equipped to understand Confirmation as a personal commitment. At the same time, I've always been glad that the rudiments of the faith were drilled into me. This provided me with certainty and hope at many difficult times in my life, especially in the crises that crouched around the next corner.

□ □ □

My peaceful, happy childhood was disturbed by illness when I was about twelve years old. I returned home from a Boy Scout retreat with pneumonia and what the doctors suspected was rheumatic fever. I was sicker than I probably knew for a number of months and missed virtually all of eighth grade. After I regained my strength the first time, I had a relapse, and our doctor became worried about the condition of my heart. He ordered that I not participate in any sports. When I entered U of D High (University of Detroit High School, now called University of Detroit Jesuit High School and Academy), I was allowed to climb the stairs to the freshman and sophomore classrooms only once a day.

This was especially frustrating because I'd always had amazing stamina; I really didn't pay much attention to the doctors' orders except when under the direct supervision of my parents or the school. Still, the inactivity led to weight gain, and I became a pudgy kid, which I hated. What's more, the physical isolation my illness brought with it became an emotional isolation. Like my father, I took refuge in books, becoming a voracious reader. I liked history and novels especially, and, as I often had trouble sleeping, I would grab a book and read long into the night.

My mother worried over me because of my health, of course, and that added to my brothers' and sisters' complaints that I was being spoiled. One time, Hilary was especially upset with me. We were arguing, and my mother admonished him to lay off me.

"He's turning into a spoiled jerk," Hilary insisted.

"Look at me," she replied. "You've had a mother. He's not going to have a mother. Leave him alone."

Anyone could see by her pallor that her health was in decline. Indeed, her heart condition was growing rapidly worse. I vividly remember the night she died, April 11, 1955. It was Easter night. Sonny, a senior, and Hilary, a junior in medical school, were attending to her. They were talking on the phone to her doctor, their voices rising and becoming more strained as they followed his instructions with little effect. I came into her room while this was going on and heard Sonny yell into the phone, "I've already given her a shot of adrenaline and it's not working!"

I looked at her, propped up on two pillows. I asked her, "Mama, what's wrong?"

She was always a very prayerful woman, and she chose to answer in the only way she could. She took out her rosary from between the pillows and with her thumb held up the crucifix to me. That was the last thing she did. I was fifteen years old.

My father had always revered and worshipped my mother. He mourned her loss terribly. It so happened, as well, that her death came as the nest was about to empty. Long before my mother's final illness, Margaret Claire and Sonny each had been planning their weddings. Both were married and gone within two months of my mother's death. Hilary left for the University of Pennsylvania to begin his residency in surgery. The following year, Agnes Cecile married as well.

My father never had many friends. He didn't go out with the boys, and he drank hardly at all. For many years, he had lived a life of heroic, if quiet, sacrifice as he devoted himself to his wife and children. Our at-home family of seven had quickly dwindled to two.

Within a year after my mother's death, my father and I fell into a grim Sunday regimen. We would go to Mass at ten o'clock, then drive to the cemetery, where my father would weep so uncontrollably that I would have to drive us home.

I was very lonely, but also very religious. We had Mass every day at U of D High, and that was important to me. I thought long and hard about becoming a priest.

Every day, when school let out at 2:35, I would stop by the chapel once more. I'd sit there and talk to my mother and pray, then hitchhike or take the bus home to an empty house, which was difficult.

I was fortunate to have my sisters and brothers and good friends to lean on. They made up much of what was lacking at home. Margaret Claire became like a second mom; as the eldest she had always nurtured me. When she married two months after my mother died, she and her husband, Russ Hastings, rented a small apartment only two or three miles from where we lived. She was extremely good to me, providing a desperately needed last dose of mothering.

I would often ride over to their apartment on my bike. Margaret Claire taught me manners, particularly how to behave around young women — a subject of increasing interest. She also taught me how to dance. She would put "Peg of My Heart" and the other romantic ballads of the midfifties on her old phonograph and show me how to glide with my partner around the dance floor. She'd let me cadge a cigarette from her pack now and again, but "only one," she'd say, keeping to a motherly moderation.

Margaret Claire had worked as an executive secretary before marriage and would later raise seven children of her own. Russ was a CPA and became comptroller of Dodge Truck. They were the first among my family members to enter a whole new socioeconomic class.

Within eighteen months of my mother's death, I underwent a transformation that was partly physical, certainly emotional, and had unexpected spiritual extensions. I began to realize that my brothers and sisters were off making their own lives. I felt that I was completely on my own and that I would rise or fall on my own strength. My father's admonition that I take my success into my own hands became an implacable necessity. At the deepest level, I decided that I was going to live my life and not be a victim. I wasn't going to feel sorry for myself. I was going to carve out my own life, whatever it took. I began hardening myself and maturing swiftly.

Between my junior and senior years of high school, I determined not to be fat anymore. I fasted, eating sparingly, all summer while working as a house painter in the sticky Detroit heat. My last growth spurt hit at the same time, taking me over the six-foot mark. I lost thirty pounds and grew about four inches. When I came back to school for my senior year, people hardly recognized me. The following summer, when I was working as a scaffold painter with a crew of older men, they took to calling me "Six O'clock," because I was as thin and straight as clock hands at six o'clock.

Losing so much weight renewed my confidence and helped me reconnect with the tremendous stamina and energy I'd known as a child. I felt powerful and ready to meet life's demands—on my own terms.

Chapter Two

Love Across the Divide

Three years after my mother died, as I was about to enter college, my father remarried. I might have seen this coming, because a year or so before, the Sunday routine for my father and me changed. We still went to Mass and to the cemetery, but when we came home, my father would say, "I'll see you later." I would be alone for the rest of the day while he visited a widow who lived a few doors from us.

This woman's family had a sad history. Two years before my mother died, her husband had died tragically, and my parents had talked about how sorry they felt for her. She had one son a little younger than I was. Over time, my father and the widow, Clara, grew fond of each other.

There was no announcement of their engagement or impending marriage. I came home from college one day, and my father introduced me to his new wife, simple as that. Needless to say, I wasn't thrilled about this, and my sisters struggled to accept the new marriage as well. As a freshman in college, I made it a policy to spend as little time at home as possible, although I did room at home through my college years. My father allowed me to keep my own hours, and we talked about nothing but sports when we bumped into each other.

Still, I knew that my father loved me. Through all the struggles of being the stepson and the difficult time I had with loneliness and with feeling somewhat abandoned, I never felt unloved and, consequently, never felt rebellious.

When I entered college at the University of Detroit, I began playing cards more seriously, as well as going to the racetrack. I played poker every Friday night, and because I have a good memory and a knack for calculating percentages on the fly, I won more than I lost. A good friend and I used our heads to do the same thing at a harness racing track. The trick was to play conservatively. We used to handicap the trotters ourselves and wait until the seventh race—when anyone could enter the local racetrack free—to start placing bets. We made only six-dollar win, place, or show bets, which gave us the greatest chance of making a percentage. We never went for a kill, only a percentage. As I made money from cards and the track, I bought bonds to avoid blowing the money.

In college, drinking was common, the parties got wild, and the fights drew not only blood but also the police. My Catholic training stood me in good stead, though. I prided myself in being moderate in drinking and walking away from trouble when I saw it developing. The hardness in me was directed to productive ends.

Toward the end of my freshman year, my father noticed that I never seemed to be short of spending money. "Where do you get all this money?" he asked. "You never seem to be short."

"Well, Dad," I said, "I'm very good at cards." I didn't have the courage to tell him about the racetrack.

"No, no, no, I don't want you doing that anymore," he said, "even if you are good at it. You'll get beat up one day or worse. You have to promise me, Mike, that you'll stop."

I wasn't happy about it, but I promised—and then honored that promise out of my great respect for him.

I had one friend with a rebellious streak. He compiled so many demerits that he was kicked out of U of D High and thereafter became, of course, a priest. When we were eighteen years old, we double-dated the night before he was to enter seminary college. We took the girls, who lived on the other side of town, home early. Then we stopped and bought a couple of beers, storing them in the back seat for later.

At a stoplight, a convertible pulled up beside us. The driver was a very cute girl, and her friend had blonde hair that tumbled over her shoulders. The flirty driver gunned the engine, daring us to race. The light turned green, and we took off . . . only to be pulled over moments later by a policeman, who then spotted the beer in the back seat.

We were arrested and taken to the Grosse Pointe Shores police station. I called home, so scared that the policeman had to explain the situation. This must have sent my father instantly over the moon, because I heard the policeman shouting, "No, no, no! He's not dead! He's not dead! Sir, he's not dead!" The policeman rolled his eyes. "It's only that he's been caught with beer in the car."

A month later, my father, my friend, and I had to go to night court, a scene that played like the opening of a Mickey Rooney movie. Dad got up before the judge and said, "This is a good boy. His mother died, and he's never been any trouble."

It sounded as if my father were trying to keep me out of Sing Sing, and the court erupted in laughter.

The judge made my friend and me write out the ordinance fifty times—that was it. Before the sentencing, he inquired about what we were doing with our lives. He wanted to know where we went to school.

My friend said, "Sacred Heart Seminary."

"You're becoming a priest and you're riding around Detroit drinking beer?" the judge asked.

Once again, the court broke up.

□ □ □

Cards on the weekends, evenings at the track, chasing girls, and working odd jobs left little time for studying during my freshman year at the University of Detroit. I passed all my classes but hardly with distinction. The university was expensive, and I began thinking of transferring to Wayne State University.

Wayne State was an urban university with more than thirty thousand students. It had a tremendous chemistry program and a medical school, and as my father had virtually preordained that I would be heading into medicine, I decided to make the switch.

At Wayne State, I took two majors: chemistry and political science. I greatly enjoyed the political science and related history classes. I had to work much harder at chemistry, although the sciences had their own fascination.

In my junior year, I took a job at a pharmacy, where I was eventually allowed to set my own hours. I loved the pharmacy because I liked working with people and the feeling of having a small hand in solving their problems. Because of my chemistry major, I was allowed to fill prescriptions like today's technical assistants. I'd even get calls from doctors, asking, "Can you give me a little advice here? What's the latest tranquilizer on the market? What are the other doctors giving for the flu?"

The pharmacy where I worked, Wilson & Wolfer, had a large mail-order business selling vitamin E. Whenever I needed to work a few extra hours, I could always go in and make up packages.

I started taking vitamin E and have always sworn by it. My know-it-all doctor brothers joked that I had "the most expensive urine in town."

One day in a cafeteria next to the Wayne State campus, I was captivated by the sight of a young woman. She was beautiful and held herself with dignity and sophistication—clearly more mature and self-possessed than those around her. She was a lady in the true sense of that old-fashioned word. I wanted to marry her before I knew her name. Who was she?

As a junior at Wayne State, I had little or no spending money. I lived at home and took my meals there. Eating lunch at the cafeteria was a luxury, but that was the only place I knew I could spot this enchanting young woman. So I contrived lunches by mixing hot water and ketchup packets and buying a soda to ward off the proprietor. One of my friends was familiar with her crowd, and I asked him to find out her name.

"Nancy Lupe," he later reported.

That it was a Spanish name didn't compute, although that hardly mattered. I badgered my friend until he finally introduced us.

Her name turned out to be Lauppe, a German name derived from the word for *arbor*. I asked her out immediately, and wonder of wonders, she said yes.

I asked her to what was known then as a Notre Dame party—the rave of the time. Notre Dame parties were held at out-of-the-way locations, live bands played, and five to six hundred people showed up—most of them liquored up.

The party was BYOB, and I asked if Nancy would like something to drink. She didn't drink to speak of, but she thought a gin and Squirt might be all right. I stopped at a liquor store and bought a pint of gin with an ID I had "adapted" from my brother's draft card. (It was never hard for underage kids to buy alcohol in Detroit.)

At the party, I made up Nancy's gin and Squirt and took a Coke for myself.

"Why aren't you drinking?" she asked.

I explained that I had an ulcer and my doctor had warned me off it.

"Then why did you buy anything for me?" she asked, looking at me as if I had just jabbed her with an elbow.

Unfortunately and embarrassingly, every girl I'd ever dated came up to us that night and gave me a boisterous "Hi, Mike!" My old friends from high school were there with their dates, and Nancy immediately liked my crowd. She told me later that she appreciated how close my friends and I were and yet how accepting of her.

When the dancing that night reached a frenzy, some of the fellows, not knowing how to ratchet up the energy otherwise, started ripping the bathroom fixtures out of the walls. I got us out of there.

I took Nancy home to Grosse Pointe. It was a clear night, the stars dotting the sky. As we stood close on her parents' driveway, she peered up over my right shoulder and said, "Oh, look, there's Orion. And there's Cassio—" Before she could call the constellation's name, I had kissed her, and from that moment on I have been as deeply in love with Nancy as a man can be with a woman.

For another year or so afterward, Nancy had reservations, even conflicting commitments. At the time I'd taken her out, she was also dating a fraternity boy at the University of Michigan. They had begun seeing each other in high school, and Nancy assumed, as did her boyfriend, that they would marry one day.

But he was at the University of Michigan, she was at Wayne State, and she meant to keep a few options open.

We got on so well together that our relationship quickly threatened to become serious, even in her mind. To avoid the conclusion that she should tell her University of Michigan beau about me, Nancy broke up with me three times. "I don't think we should see each other anymore," she'd say.

"Fine," I'd say. Then I would date the best-looking girls I could possibly find in order to make her jealous, which worked.

During our courtship, I tried to be ardent without being pushy. I brought her flowers, candy, and knickknacks from the pharmacy—anything that would assure her of my love. We had long, long talks, which in the end won her heart.

☐ ☐ ☐

As my graduation from Wayne State neared, I began thinking about whether I really wanted to go to medical school. I saw that medicine was the perfect fit for Sonny. He was already a well-known cardiologist. And Hilary was totally consumed with becoming a fine surgeon. My father had convinced me that the professions were the way to go. But medicine? I liked my political science classes far more than the hard sciences. I began thinking about going to law school.

When I asked myself what I truly wanted to do with my life, I found that I wanted to be a builder. I didn't understand very well what that might mean or why that answer came to mind so insistently. I had dreamed as a child of using the bricks from my mother's family's yards for my own constructions, and perhaps I'd inherited the entrepreneurial spirit of the O'Reillys. The dynamic life of post-war Detroit, where much of the new wealth of the

1950s was generated, certainly must have been an influence. I found myself intrigued by the way the pharmacy was growing its business through its mail-order sideline and similar instances of entrepreneurship.

Beyond whatever environmental and family influences I might cite, though, I'd have to say that I simply sensed my true calling, my vocation. Something in me wanted to be a builder—of business, society, or government. Maybe all three. Law school seemed the best way to begin. With my background in chemistry, I thought I might specialize in chemical and other scientific patents—at least at the beginning.

I went to my father and told him of my plans to attend law school at Wayne State. He was even more disappointed than I had imagined. He ended the conversation by snapping, "All right! You can become a garbage collector, for all I care."

This caused a rift that took years to heal. In fairness, my father didn't trouble me about the decision further. He simply washed his hands of the matter. In turn, I became more determined to set my own course, although I longed like all sons for my father's approval.

At about the same time in 1961, Nancy and I were engaged to be married. Her parents had always treated me with great kindness. Her father, Fred, was a reserved, stiff man of German descent, but nevertheless cordial. Her mother was always warm to me. Their manner changed markedly, though, once I asked Nancy's father for his daughter's hand.

Fred was one of the finest men I've ever known—a doctor, practicing the old specialty Eye, Ear, Nose, and Throat. He saw his practice as a way of serving people and always scaled his fees according to a patient's ability to pay. He even treated people for free.

The thought of Nancy marrying an Irish Catholic unnerved Fred. A nominal Christian, he had raised his family in the Episcopal Church. Though my future father-in-law didn't have dogmatic religious views, he acted strictly on the guidance of his conscience and the truth he knew. What Fred did possess in full measure, unhappily, were the common prejudices of the time against Catholics — and the bad information that supported them. He longed to save his daughter from the life he foresaw of drudgery and superstition. As our wedding neared, he actually started taking tranquilizers to maintain his composure. He called Nancy "Princess," and in his fear I think Fred imagined her reduced to an Irish scullery maid with twenty-seven children.

I was nervous when I asked permission to wed his daughter, and I didn't communicate clearly that I expected us to marry in the Catholic Church. When her family began to make plans for an Episcopal ceremony, I made myself clear. Nancy's father replied that he would never set foot in a Catholic Church.

My determination to be married within the Church had nothing to do with my own family's expectations. My father recognized immediately what a lady Nancy was. Hilary teased that I was marrying Nancy "because she's from Grosse Pointe and has money." Margaret Claire pretended to be outraged: "Well, you know you're going to go to hell because you're marrying a Protestant." But my family saw how good Nancy would be for me and blessed the match.

I was insistent on marrying in the Catholic Church because I couldn't conceive of living my life apart from it. Nancy and I knew we were united in the core beliefs of the Christian faith, and she found worshipping with me natural after being raised an Episcopalian, with its nearly identical liturgy. At the same time, I never asked Nancy to convert to Catholicism. I knew she was a better Christian than I was, and I left it to her own conscience as to which communion she wanted to be a part of. I understood how hurtful it would have been to Nancy's parents for her to convert.

Nancy's mother, Priscilla, had a great deal of practical wisdom. While we were going through this tense period before our wedding, she sat Nancy down and told her that she must face squarely whatever consequences came from marrying a poor Irish Catholic. If that was Nancy's decision, though, her parents would still love her. Priscilla realized that it would probably be natural for Nancy to become a Catholic at some point. She asked her to wait a long time, preferably until her father died.

With her family's difficulties in reconciling themselves to our wedding, Nancy and I made a decision about which we still feel ambivalent. I went to see my parish priest and told him my predicament. He arranged for us to get married secretly in Toledo.

Saturday morning, June 25, 1962, we drove to Toledo and were married by a Jesuit priest at St. Mary's. The brief ceremony took place in the church's breezeway with the gardener and his wife as witnesses.

We drove straight back to Detroit. Nancy dropped me off at work, and I spent the next eight hours filling vitamin E orders, not even seeing Nancy until the next day. We said nothing about the wedding to anyone.

Four days later, we were married again in my in-laws' living room by a judge who was a friend of her family, with just her parents, her godmother, and her brothers present. No reception followed. It was a tense, difficult time.

Thereafter, Nancy and I never talked about religion with her family. We never talked about it even though Nancy and I went to her parents' house for dinner nearly every Sunday afternoon.

At the time, this seemed to be the only way to get along. In retrospect, I can see that the tension between Catholics and Protestants, which would have a continuing influence on my life, affected us more than I understood. As I would begin to understand more about the Christian faith, I would see that much of this tension is due to Catholics misunderstanding what Protestants believe and Protestants misunderstanding what Catholics believe.

When Nancy and I married, I had about a hundred dollars in my pocket, law school ahead, and a part-time job at a pharmacy. Fortunately, Nancy secured a job as a high-school English teacher and agreed to work while I went through law school. That was another thing that upset her father — that she would be supporting us. As she pointed out, though, I would be working as many hours as she, plus going to law school, which is exactly what I did.

I remember the dean of Wayne State Law School welcoming the students "to one of the two oldest professions — and of the two, the least respected." As Dick the Butcher says in Shakespeare's *Henry VI*, "The first thing we do, let's kill all the lawyers."

Law school was a bracing intellectual challenge. This was the major leagues, and I was determined to excel. From high school on, I knew that I was bright enough, although my performance had never been equal to my ability, a source of complaint from my father. He had drilled into us the Puritan work ethic, but I never had a great enough sense of purpose to embrace that ethic totally. Married, I could no longer afford dilly-dallying.

Fortunately, I had made the right choice: I liked law school immediately. I plunged into the *tuml* of it (a Yiddish word that means "commotion"), the swirl of activity that goes with the adversarial nature of the law. I saw quickly that society can dispense with many things, but never the rule of law, without which every type of civil relationship begins disintegrating—an insight that any trip to the Third World brings home.

I wasn't at law school a week before I knew that I would never be a patent attorney. Every aspect of business law appealed powerfully to me, and I began to glimpse how my calling to be a "builder" might be realized. The law made the building of society possible. I wanted more security than my father knew, but making money never motivated me. The prospect of being a business lawyer and enabling enterprises to go forward was more compelling.

My newfound love of the law activated my energies as never before. I got up every morning at 4:30 and studied until my first class at 8:30. Classes generally lasted until the early afternoon. As soon as my classes were over for the day, I headed to the pharmacy and worked there until nine. Then I'd go home and have dinner with Nancy. In the couple of hours we had to spend together, we'd talk, and sometimes I'd help her grade papers or look over the next day's studies. I was friendly with my fellow students, but I didn't have time to socialize. They would go have a beer and I would go to work. If I wasn't studying or working, I felt restless and lazy.

By the end of my first year in law school, I was on scholarship, ranked sixth in my class of about two hundred, and had won cash awards from textbook publishers for finishing first in particular courses. In my second and third years of law school, I was first in my class. I was elected to Wayne *Law Review* and left the pharmacy in my senior year to begin working as a law clerk.

During the same year, Nancy and I bought a house in Grosse Pointe Farms. We'd lived so frugally that we were able to make a down payment of six thousand dollars on a house that cost sixteen thousand. Nancy's father supplied the rest in a mortgage.

The house was very small but cherished. The neighbors—mostly young professionals, dentists, pediatricians, CPAs, or small-business owners—were so friendly that most mornings when I was headed downtown, someone would stop and give me a ride before I reached the bus stop.

In addition to our other activities, Nancy and I began remodeling the house. After I came home from work at nine, I worked, painting every room and sanding every floor. This went on for months, and now I marvel at how we fit that into the schedule.

The new house and having us close by pleased Nancy's father, but he was still not reconciled to the marriage. During my law school years, he would introduce us by saying, "This is my daughter, Nancy, and this is her husband, Mr. Timmis." The way he said "Mr. Timmis" made our marriage sound suspicious. I used to get so angry that I would tell Nancy I wasn't going to her parents' house anymore. Then she would calm me down. I'd realize that she was his only daughter, his "Princess," and that she had paid a price to marry me. So we'd keep our usual Sundays with the in-laws. I respected Nancy's parents so much I did not grow resentful, despite my Irish temper.

My in-laws attended the Honors Convocation when I graduated from law school, and it turned out to be a pivotal moment in our relationship. During the ceremony, I kept being called to the platform to receive various awards. Finally, the dean said, "This is a very special night for me because of an honored guest in the audience." Nancy saw a State Supreme Court judge start to preen in anticipation of his name being called. But the dean meant Nancy's father, who had operated on the dean, restoring his eyesight. He asked Dr. Lauppe to stand, and everyone gave him a vigorous round of applause.

Then the dean said, "I just want you to know, Dr. Lauppe,

that in all my years I have never had a finer student than your son-in-law, Michael Timmis."

From that night on, I became "Mike" to my father-in-law.

Chapter Three

Success . . . and Its Sacrifices

During the last months of law school, in the spring of 1965, I began looking for a position at a firm where I could practice business law. I was particularly interested in small- and medium-sized businesses, although a lucrative offer from Chrysler Corporation nearly persuaded me otherwise.

I asked one of my law school professors, Harold Marchant, if he thought I should take Chrysler's offer. He had been in private practice and was someone I truly respected. "Sure," he said, "if you want to be a kept man. But I think you have a lot more to offer."

So I turned down an eye-popping starting salary. I then interviewed at the firm where I had already started to clerk, Marco & Marco. It was led by its patriarch, Paul Marco, who had founded the practice in 1940. He spent half the year in Florida. So I was interviewed by his brother Philip. Philip was an ex-Marine who had fought at Guadalcanal and the other great Pacific island battles during World War II. He was a man's man, and I immediately gravitated toward him. He liked my profile: a young Catholic from a family of modest means who had made a fashionable marriage. Status was very important to Marco & Marco. When he asked me to join the firm, I accepted gladly.

What sold me on Marco & Marco was its entrepreneurial approach. The firm not only practiced law but also functioned as a holding company that acquired and sold businesses. When the firm bought a business, the partners and even the associates would be given a percentage of the business's equity, albeit small.

For instance, early in my career, Marco & Marco bought a cemetery, which can be a surprisingly profitable business. I received something like a 1 percent stake in this cemetery, with the firm financing 100 percent of the purchase price. Leverage was king in those days. When Marco & Marco sold the cemetery, I received a bonus of about thirty thousand dollars. For a young couple like Nancy and me, that was a huge amount of money, and indeed it's still a lot today. Being part of the firm meant that in addition to my salary, I'd be receiving substantial bonuses along the way, and I'd learn about business from the standpoint of ownership.

This came at a cost. Paul Marco and his partners were intent on being the best small legal firm in Detroit. There were four partners and another associate when I was hired. That meant everyone worked six days a week and carried a briefcase home for Sunday afternoon. I began working twelve-hour days, and I added to my responsibilities as an associate by teaching legal writing to minorities at Wayne State and beginning a master's degree in taxation.

After graduating from law school, I presumed I was already one heck of a lawyer. It didn't take long, however, to realize I didn't know anything. I started learning all over again as fast as I could. I ultimately abandoned my master's studies in taxation because the learning curve at the firm was far steeper and more important.

One of my first hurdles, of course, was passing the bar. The firm didn't make any provision for me to take the usual preparatory class in the summer, so I bought study guides and crammed. The night before the exam was to be given at the University of Michigan, I drove to Ann Arbor. A classmate and I went out to dinner and ordered steak, which we downed with a bottle of wine. I wasn't worried at all. I was at the top of my class; I was going to pass the bar. A whole day and a half off from work, even if it meant writing essays in response to exam questions, seemed too good to be true. It was almost like a holiday.

Most of the candidates I took the bar with felt differently. I remember having to find an alternate restroom because so many taking the exam were throwing up from anxiety.

I did have a few nervous moments later, as the firm's partners warned darkly that I would have to leave if I didn't pass. (In reality, I'm sure they would have let me take it again; I was way too good at all the grunt work they were throwing my way.)

The results appeared in the newspaper just before Christmas of 1965. But I couldn't find my name. Much to my dismay, Nancy scanned the paper too and finally found my name—my results had been listed under Grosse Pointe rather than Detroit. I'd passed! Her family was overjoyed, and we all went off together that evening to celebrate. I was formally admitted to the bar on January 2, 1966.

□ □ □

Before long, the other associate at the firm took another job, and I was left to service the needs of four partners for research, memoranda, and filings. My early years at the firm became an increasingly unhappy time in which I could never do enough; pleasing my bosses seemed humanly impossible. They prided themselves on being the hardest-working, toughest SOBs anywhere, and I wasn't about to let them or anyone else beat me at that game. I was going to be unstoppable, a pro, whatever it took.

Our new life wasn't what Nancy had expected. My position

allowed her to leave teaching, but she saw even less of me than in my days at law school. Those three years of toil were supposed to have led to a better life. Was that what we were living? She was beginning to think she didn't know me. At first we did find the time to be part of the Catholic Family Movement—a lay group in which young couples in the neighborhood got together after dinner for a time of fellowship. But such activities were soon displaced by the all-consuming demands of work.

Then our son, Michael Jr. was born on April 27, 1966. I'd always wanted to be a father—a great father. I used to lie in bed thinking about it. Though I wasn't about to realize my father-in-law's fears and burden Nancy with twenty-seven children, I did hope for a large family. So the moment Mike was born was absolutely joyful. This was the beginning—and oh, what a precious one!

Michael was born in the middle of the night, and afterward I went over to see my dad. He had been given a bottle of good whiskey, Crown Royal, by my Uncle Bill, and we sat at the kitchen table sharing a drink. For that one moment, with the birth of my son, my own personal world seemed completely reconciled—both sides of the family happy, a lifetime dream come true, and a future filled with the love I instantly felt for my son.

I took the day off to be with Nancy and baby Michael. Believe it or not, my bosses gave me hell for it. "Why didn't you come to work?" they demanded.

I said, "My son was born—my first child."

"Well, so what?" they replied.

□ □ □

Although the law firm's demands could be punishing, I enjoyed the actual practice of the law from the very beginning, even when most of my time was taken up with paperwork. Once I began working more directly with clients, I found the long hours easier to sustain. I loved my clients. As a lawyer, I met with people at crucial stages in their lives and often became their confidant. If they needed me, I would be there—I didn't care what time of day or night it was. Just as I'd enjoyed helping people at the pharmacy, I loved helping my legal clients.

As dedicated and skilled as I was, I realized I wasn't anything special. There were a lot of smart lawyers. No one can ever promise a client that his opinion will prevail. At the beginning, I couldn't pretend to have much experience or the resources of a large firm to back me up. What I could promise my clients was that I would never stop fighting for them. I came to see myself as a juggernaut: I was going to keep coming and coming, and there was no way anyone could stop me. Sometimes I'd look across a negotiating table at opposing counsel and see their frustration. They weren't willing to pay the price in sheer work hours I was, and opponents often settled on favorable terms rather than counter my adamant representation.

The smallness of most Detroit firms compared to those in Chicago and New York allowed me a more multifaceted view of business law. I'd take business trips to New York and other cities, where I'd ask for a break in negotiations by saying, "Let me talk to my pension guy about that and I'll get back to you." Of course, *I* was my pension guy, so I'd think about the matter for a while and then walk back into the sessions with a proposal. "Here's what my pension guy says. . . ." Working in all aspects of business law proved particularly helpful when I began branching out into business myself.

As I've said, I was the only associate in a firm with four partners for a while, and the partner for whom I did the most work thought he invented the law. He was a perfectionist and had a nasty side. He enjoyed reading me the riot act. As my knowledge and skills improved, his berating became gratuitous and finally insufferable. I had grown up in a tougher neighborhood than he understood.

Our offices were on the twenty-second floor of the Penobscot Building, and I was there working overtime one night when my nemesis breezed back in from a business trip. He walked into my office, threw a contract I had composed on my desk, and shouted, "This is a piece of [expletive]!"

I stood up, went to my door, and closed it. Instead of responding to his tirade, I walked straight to him and grabbed him around the neck. He was stockier, but I was taller, younger, and stronger. "I'm going to throw you out that [expletive] window," I said through clenched teeth.

His face instantly drained of color.

I continued, "I've had enough of *your* [expletive]. I don't care what you think, I'm going to kill you."

I kept a hold on his neck and pushed him over by the window. At that moment, I didn't care if I went to jail for the rest of my life. I have never been in a rage like that before or since. "Do you want me to throw you out that window, you so-and-so?" I said. "Don't you ever, ever, *ever* say anything like that to me again!"

Once I had explained the terms of the "new contract" to him, my rage began to subside. I let go of his neck.

My adversary never spoke that way to me again. I'm not exactly proud of this episode, but I see it as a last rite of passage: I finally knew my worth, both as a lawyer and a human being.

After about two years, my father-in-law became so concerned

about how I was being treated at the firm that he made me an incredibly generous offer. "These people are using you up, Mike," he said. "You are working so hard. You have the gift. You will be successful. I think you should leave the law firm and start your own practice. I will back you for two years. By that time, you will be on your way."

I said, "Dad, I really appreciate that, but I've got to do it by myself."

I felt a tremendous amount of affection toward him for making the offer. By that time, Nancy's parents had really become parents to me, and I loved them dearly. While I turned down the offer, I certainly agreed with his opinion about how I was being used. I became so resentful that I resolved that once I was asked to be a partner, I would resign. That would show them.

Because of the special rapport I'd developed with clients, I began to build up my own client base and to increase the amount of business that various enterprises sent Marco & Marco's way. Clients we had been billing five or six thousand dollars a year grew to fifty thousand–dollar accounts. I was turning into a rainmaker. This attracted the attention of other firms, which approached me with partnership offers. I was on the verge of accepting one of these when I asked my eldest brother's advice.

"Mike, don't leave," Sonny said. "The grass is always greener on the other side. All the stuff you put up with at your current firm you're going to put up with in some other firm."

I was still torn when, one day in late 1970, the firm called. "We're going to make you a partner." I was truly surprised. Normally, it took seven or eight years for an associate to be offered a partnership, and I had been with the firm for only five. My thoughts of throwing the offer in their faces went straight out the window. I had been made a partner!

My joy at my new partnership soon gave way to life's unending complications, of course. As it happened, the first year I was a partner I earned thirty-five thousand dollars. I had actually been making more as an associate, and the reduction blistered me. I raised Cain in a meeting until I was given another bump.

The great anticipated moments in life rarely provide lasting satisfaction, do they? I remained restless and longed for ever greater success.

Chapter Four

Walking Through Walls

In 1969, I was standing on the street corner outside the law firm's downtown offices early one evening, waiting for a ride home. An accountant named Randy Agley, whom I had worked with at Arthur Andersen, wheeled around the corner and rolled down his window. "What are you doing?" he called out.

"Waiting for a ride," I said. "I think my friend has forgotten me."

Randy offered me a ride and asked if I'd like to swing by the house he was buying in Grosse Pointe Park.

"Sure, I'd love to see it," I replied.

As he told me about the house, I caught his enthusiasm for the property and the comforts it would bring his family. I offered to handle the closing as a professional courtesy. Randy already had another lawyer helping out, but he was grateful for the offer.

Randy's lawyer had to be out of town the day of the closing, however, and he called me at the last minute to see if I would pinch hit. I agreed. That evening on my way home from work, I dropped by the property and walked through it. I noticed a swimming pool had been recently installed.

That made me wonder if any mechanic's liens had been

filed—unpaid debts that would belong to Randy if the seller hadn't disclosed their existence. I looked up the records and found sixty thousand dollars in liens that the title company had missed. Having to assume the liens would have been disastrous for Randy. He was grateful for the help and began recommending my services to his accounting clients.

As a result, we began working more closely together, particularly on mergers and acquisitions. Randy was better with numbers than anyone I'd ever seen; he could do complex computations in his head while others were still searching for their calculators. He liked my aggressiveness and my ability to break down complex transactions to their fundamental issues. Together we made a terrific team.

In one instance, Randy had a client who wanted to sell a landfill he owned in the Detroit area. The client was hoping to move the property for approximately a quarter of a million dollars. The huge waste management companies we know today were then being established, so the major players were snapping up smaller companies as they tried to dominate geographic regions and gain market share. Randy and I understood the direction in which the industry was heading and, most importantly, how to calculate the value of a property over its useful life. We were able to prove to potential buyers that the landfill possessed a much greater value than previously expected. We sold the property for many times our client's original expectations—well in excess of a million dollars.

After the deal was completed, I said to Randy, "You know, we could make a lot of money if we could buy and sell businesses for ourselves. We have the expertise. We just need capital."

As we continued to collaborate on other projects, our desire to go into business together grew. In the meantime, the clients

Randy sent my way dramatically increased the business I brought into the law firm.

□ □ □

After Michael was born, Nancy and I looked forward to having another child. Months and then years passed. What we didn't know was that during an appendectomy Nancy had in college, the doctors found and removed a large, benign tumor from one of her ovaries. (Her mother revealed this only when she was dying of cancer, because she previously thought it might have affected our marriage.) Prior to becoming pregnant with Michael, Nancy had experienced a miscarriage. Our concerns about having a second child became acute. We both underwent tests—and their humiliations. I remember having a plastic cup unceremoniously shoved into my hand and a nurse hiking her thumb toward the office's bathroom door. This process was so insensitive I felt demeaned, and it hurt me to see Nancy feel the same way.

It took a while for the tests to be processed. In the interim we did our joyful best to conceive.

When we sat down with the doctor to review the tests, he said, "I'm sorry, but your results indicate there's almost no chance you'll have another child."

I said, "That's not the case, doctor, because Nancy thinks she's pregnant right now."

"She does?"

"She's been pregnant twice before. She ought to know the signs."

He was skeptical, but he quickly ran a test right there in the office. When he sat back down with us, he said, "You must have a lucky Buddha or something. Nancy's right. She's pregnant."

Our daughter, Laura, was born on January 14, 1970. Nancy had fast labors both times, so we barely made it to the hospital. Once again, with Laura's birth I experienced pure joy, and this time an added dose of relief and gratitude to God. There were so few girls in the family that I knew Laura's birth would strike Sonny as especially fortunate, because he had six sons.

"Sonny, Sonny," I gushed when I called him with our news, "we had a girl!"

He was so envious that all he could do was say, "You lucky SOB!" and hang up the phone.

With two children, a law partnership, and my client list growing, I felt I could walk through walls. My confidence fueled my habitually frenetic pace. I often functioned on as little as three or four hours' sleep. I'd work until nine at night and then be back in the office shortly after seven. I was living off adrenaline.

□ □ □

In the early spring of 1971, my father-in-law told me that he had a heart condition and needed a catheterization. He insisted that Sonny be his doctor; Sonny was the best, he reasoned. I wanted the best for the man I now called Dad as well.

The Sunday before Fred was scheduled for his heart catheterization, Nancy and I and the kids had dinner with my in-laws as usual. I could tell that Dad was tense, thinking of the next day's procedure. I didn't know how worried he was until he called us back into the house from the car. It was a cold, spring Sunday, and the kids were bundled up in winter coats, but I could tell from his manner, as he tapped on the window and motioned us to come back into the house, that he had something important to tell me.

Nancy and I went in the house by ourselves, and Fred said to me, "I'm not going to survive this catheterization."

"Dad," I said, trying to be reassuring, "Sonny does these procedures every day. It's strictly routine. You'll be fine. You're a doctor. You should know that."

"Ordinarily, you'd be right," he said. "But I have a bad feeling about this."

"Well, that's natural."

His eyes appealed to me. "I want you to do a couple of things for me."

"Whatever you need. You know that."

"In a minute, I want you to share a toast with me," he said. "Someone gave me a bottle of champagne when I returned from World War II, and I never opened it. I'm afraid it's warm, but I want to share a toast all the same."

I nodded, waiting for him to reveal what he most needed.

"And I want you to see to my affairs. Make sure my sons and Priscilla are taken care of," he said. "And wind up the practice."

"Of course I'll help. When and if the need does arise. I imagine Nancy and her brothers—"

"No, I want *you* to manage things. You're the leader in this family. I'd like your promise." His mouth was taut, his face drawn and blanched.

"You have it," I said.

He was looking at me steadily. "Okay, good." He took a breath. "Now let's have that drink."

The next day, I was at a lunch for lawyers participating in a softball league when I was called to the phone. I was needed at the hospital. My father-in-law's premonition couldn't possibly have come true, could it? I was racing down the hospital hall when one of the doctors I knew called out, "No need to run. He's already dead." That's the way I found out about Dad's death—as hard and as cold as that.

I lived a very different life from my "second dad." Fred Lauppe was an orderly German. The discipline of his life, rather than being hard to bear, made room for love. He was out the door at six o'clock every morning for rounds at Harpers Hospital. He kept office hours until midafternoon. On his way home, he stopped once more at the hospital to see his patients. During Nancy's growing-up years, her father sat down no later than 6:15 every evening to have dinner with his family. Afterward, he spent time with his wife, discussing his patients, the children, her household concerns, family events coming up, holidays—all the elements of living a full life that many men give short shrift.

When I first joined the law firm, its patriarch told me that I should never discuss business with my wife, because she could say something, however inadvertently, in a social context that could have a devastating effect on the business. So, as consumed with work as I was, I talked to Nancy about virtually none of it. And as pressured as I usually felt, I had little patience for her concerns and worries. By the time of Fred's passing, Nancy and I had fallen into a pattern where she fed me and left me alone, which left her incredibly isolated amid the demands of our two small children. I fulfilled my overt promises to my father-in-law, but I wished I had paid much more heed to the implicit call of his example.

Nancy's mother survived her husband by only four years. Priscilla was a wonderful, vivacious, personable, and sensitive woman. While I struggled to gain Fred's approval at the beginning of our marriage, in a very short time Priscilla began mothering me. We grew into a close, loving relationship. She had been a nurse when she met Nancy's dad, and they had the happiest marriage of any two people I've met. Priscilla's passing was a huge loss to Nancy, as well as to me, as her mother's presence a short drive away compensated, to a degree, for my increasing absence. Priscilla was the voice of reason in every family dust-up, and her advice, as direct as it could be, was always tempered by kindness.

Something had to be done with the Lauppes' home, and so, after providing due compensation to Nancy's brothers, we moved there ourselves. In this way, nine-year-old Michael and five-year-old Laura shared in the goodness of that home and its treasury of memories.

□ □ □

In the early 1970s, my friend and colleague Randy Agley was doing a lot of work for three partners, Harold Stern, Mel Garb, and Dr. Louis Imerman, who owned a collection of McDonald's franchises. The three were phenomenally successfully at this, and they came to own approximately twenty-six McDonald's restaurants, primarily in the upper Midwest. This gave them more clout than the McDonald's Corporation liked, and when they threatened to go public in a stock offering, McDonald's bought all the franchises back at a price equivalent to a public offering of stock. The three partners found themselves in the possession of approximately twenty-six million dollars.

Executives at Arthur Andersen approached these men with the idea of setting up a holding company. In other words, they recommended reinvesting the money in a variety of businesses, which would diversify their risk and likely increase their considerable wealth many times over. The three partners thought this might be a good idea, yet they weren't sure about being in business with Arthur Andersen as a whole. But they did appreciate Randy's talents, so they approached him about running a holding company for them.

Randy invited me into the new venture as the company's lawyer and a minor partner. He and I now had the capital to put our mergers and acquisitions expertise to use. So S&G Investments—for Stern and Garb, the names of our backers—came into being.

The first thing we did was buy a chain of auto parts stores, including a distribution center. I borrowed the money for my very small stake in the stores. Any legal work I did for S&G Investments I billed to the partnership. I kept a strict separation—in legal parlance, an iron gate—between my law practice and my business interests, billing S&G for my legal services.

The previous owners of the auto parts business were in their eighties. Over the years, they'd become unwilling, Randy and I thought, to make the hard decisions that could make the business highly profitable. They had too many stores in too many locations, and their inventory control needed an overhaul. Because the business owned the real estate at their locations, their poorly performing stores could be sold off. The capital from those sales could be reinvested in the business, updating the better stores and improving the operations connecting them. Randy and I also thought that new leadership could improve the performance of the workforce.

All of this might indeed have worked, except that two of the owners' sons, who had been running the business for their parents, had unwittingly negotiated with their union an unfunded past service (pension) liability of about eight hundred thousand dollars. This essentially bankrupted the company. The owners' sons had doctored the books, concealing this from us. We sued to recover what we could, and the judgment went our way, but the business had to be liquidated to cover the past pension liability and to pay off the business's creditors. The first time out of the gate, we lost S&G's and my entire investment.

We could have hurt our creditors severely, but we didn't; everyone received at least eighty-five cents on the dollar. The banks were impressed with our scrupulous repayment plan. S&G's major partners—the three McDonald's magnates—weren't happy about losing a portion of their stake, but they took it in stride. Mistakes are made in business, they reasoned; due diligence is no match for fraud. They were ready to move on to the next deal.

Our next acquisitions proved more profitable: An auto parts manufacturing business did very well for us. We bought real estate in California and Florida. We bought an oil well service completion company. We also acquired a line of drug stores, F&M Distributors, the first deep discounter in the nation.

It's often important, Randy and I have always believed, to move quickly when a deal looks right. That was the case with F&M Distributors. The owners, Fred and Margaret Cohen, had worked like slaves their whole lives, putting the business together. They wanted out—as fast as possible—and to be free of all future entanglements. There were a couple of big supermarket chains interested in buying them out too, but the chains wanted the couple to stay on for a couple of years and help with the transition. We said, "Give us ninety days and we'll pay you cash and you can leave." That made the sale for us. We did it so fast I closed it without any documentation; we supplied the closing documents after the fact. By then our relationship with our bankers was that good.

F&M Distributors became our most noteworthy company at that time. For many years after we bought it, the business supplied a great service for the communities in which it was located, employment to thousands, and cash flow that helped us scrape through elsewhere. Later it went through troubled times—everyone makes mistakes in business, including me.

Early on Randy had said to me that our successes must out-number our failures. I remember thinking we shouldn't have any failures. Even though our successes eventually far exceeded my expectations or even desires, we did experience some significant failures, and we agonized deeply over them because we knew other people were hurt by them. I can remember many nights pacing the floor in deep worry over what we were doing and how we were doing it.

As our holding company grew, S&G Investments became one of Marco & Marco's biggest clients. Even though I had carefully maintained the iron gate between my law practice and my business interests, the success of S&G must have ruffled a few feathers at Marco & Marco. Once, when the firm sold one of its businesses and I was due for one of those bonuses that had attracted me to the firm — to the tune of about two hundred thousand dollars, as I recall — my fellow partners decided to take me down a peg or two. The partner who tended to be my adversary said, "Look, Mike, you've only held your share of the equity in this business for a short time. For the rest of us, this sale has been a long time coming. We think it's inappropriate for you to participate strictly on a percentage basis." They offered me about 10 percent of what I was expecting.

"Okay," I said, "if that's the way you want to do business." I kept calm, but I was seething.

I became more resolved than ever to become a successful busi-nessman — someone whose interests couldn't be denied in this high-handed way. Such incidents, I suppose, helped transform my tough-guy façade into genuine armor plating.

Further down the road, the firm had another meeting at which the same partner who had cut my percentage of the earlier deal inquired about the firm's possible participation in the profits generated from S&G Investments. "Is there going to be something in it for us?" he asked.

"No, you've had your participation through all the hours I've billed," I said. "I'll include my younger partner, Wayne Inman, but for the rest—well, you've made your own investment decisions in the past, and now I'm making mine."

They weren't happy about it, but I was the one bringing in most of the firm's new business.

□ □ □

In 1975, the U.S. government came after both Harold Stern and Mel Garb. They had gone into an abusive tax shelter that worked like a shell game. They invested money through a Chicago law firm, whose records indicated the loss of their investment, entitling them to a tax deduction. They received a profit, however, in the same amount in a trust set up in the Cayman Islands by the same firm. A "tax straddle" like this was only legitimate if the investor's capital was at some point at risk. In this case, however, the money merely changed hands. The television program *60 Minutes* did an exposé on the case, and the government was out to make an example of high-profile tax cheats.

The IRS contacted me as the two men's attorney, and we had a meeting in my office. The agents who attended were from the IRS Intelligence Division; they had guns on their hips, which bulged prominently underneath their suit jackets. Right off the bat, they told my clients they were going to be indicted. They wanted them to plead to lesser charges and help the government pursue the principals behind the tax dodge. My clients nearly went into cardiac arrest. Their signatures were all over what had turned out to be incriminating documents.

I already knew my business partners too well, however, to believe that they were guilty of tax fraud. They listened to the people they liked and trusted and never investigated the details. They could be phenomenally flaky for such successful business-men. I had put many, many document folders before them for their signature, and they never even glanced through them. The firm in Chicago had told them this was legitimate, and that's what they believed. They were guilty of greed, yes, but not fraud. I told the IRS agents as much and ended the meeting.

I began working through the mountains of paperwork that connected my clients to the illegal enterprise and obfuscated its principals' culpability. At this point another impediment presented itself. My partners at Marco & Marco didn't want me to represent my clients; they didn't want the firm to have anything to do with the case's negative publicity. We had a knock-down, drag-out meeting, where I said, "Either I represent them or I leave."

"Well," they said, "you've never handled a criminal case."

"That's right, but these guys are innocent," I insisted. "Nobody's ever going to believe them because they've been so stupid, but that's the truth — they're innocent. I'm going to fight and I'm going to win."

Besides being in a privileged position to understand the men's innocence, I knew that anti-Semitism factored into the equation. My clients were Jewish, some of the IRS agents were Irish, and I knew they were out to stick it to my clients. As an Irishman and a Catholic myself, I was determined not to let that happen.

I spent many late nights in the office, surrounded by the case's highly complex documentation, wondering myself whether I should be handling the case. I was not an accountant, I was receiving no help from the firm, and at times I couldn't make heads or tails of the documentation. I would be sitting in my office at one o'clock in the morning, the case's papers spilling out of my hands, just weeping from exhaustion. The firm was right: I didn't have any experience handling criminal cases. I had the two men's lives in my hands. Was I doing the right thing by them? Could my pugnacity and sheer will face down the IRS's legal army?

My clients and I had to go to Miami for grand jury testimony. There the Justice Department attorneys and the IRS agents handling the case held a conference with me. Their side numbered about ten. They couldn't believe I was handling the case alone. They were going to put my clients away for as long as possible, they threatened, if I didn't counsel them to accept a plea. They wanted the lawyers and accountants who had put together the scheme. Why wouldn't my clients do the right thing—admit to their guilt and help the government put the major players away? My clients might have to do jail time, but not nearly what they would receive if the case went to trial.

"Take the deal," the agents demanded. "Take the deal!"

"It would be easy for us to take your deal," I said, "except my clients aren't guilty."

The Justice Department attorneys went ballistic. They reminded me that the IRS can investigate anyone it chooses.

Their threats pushed me over the edge. I was so enraged that I started to cry and I said, "You anti-Semitic bastards. Don't you understand? These guys are innocent, and there is no way you're going to put them in jail. I'm going to beat all of you. No matter what, I'm going to beat you. Whatever it takes, I'll work harder than any of you, and we'll win. That's a promise, a done deal, and the only one we're making."

The room went dead silent.

The grand jury soon returned indictments against the tax scheme's lawyers and its accountants, but I heard nothing about my clients' fate.

Later, on Christmas Eve of 1979, I got a call from the lead Justice Department attorney, who said, "Mike, you finally convinced us. We're not going to indict. If I'm ever in trouble, you're the first guy I'm calling."

Needless to say, my clients were thrilled. Randy went to them and said, "Look, you would have gone to jail if it weren't for him. I want him to become an equal partner in everything we're doing."

They agreed. From that time on, it was the five of us: Randy, Harold Stern, Louis Imerman, Mel Garb, and myself. That would prove extraordinarily significant within the next two years.

□ □ □

Though I'd been successful against the onslaught of the IRS, I found my home life becoming increasingly unmanageable, even though I tried to exert my will in every particular. As I became a respected figure in the community, I fell victim to self-congratulation and its accompanying imperial manner. Nancy was taking care of two little kids, and yet I insisted that the house remain spotless. I also made suggestions about how she could be a more presentable wife, including her hairstyle.

In our marriage, Nancy had grown more and more quiet. She wasn't cowed by me; she was too strong a person for that. She was disinclined to argue, however, especially because she knew that her thoughts would elicit long rebuttals. I would "lawyer" her. So she increasingly kept her mouth shut.

As I've said, our problems communicating were compounded by that standard practice of my generation of lawyers: Never tell your wife anything that she might let slip inadvertently at a social gathering. As a result, we talked about little that truly meant something to me other than the kids.

When I was unhappy, as I often was, she had no way to interpret the cause of my distress. I remember her bursting into tears one time, asking, "Is it me?"

Of course, that made me feel like a heel. "No, it's never you," I said. "It's work, honey. It's always work."

This admission didn't go very far, though, because she still had to live with the aggressive, angry, combative person I had become. My unhappiness terrified her, in part because she had no idea how to alleviate it. She just had to live with it, without any ability to address it.

Eventually, at one of our lowest points, she told me with great regret that I wasn't the man she married.

In typical fashion, I told her that was ridiculous.

She was thinking of "Six O'clock," the reed-thin, boyish-faced undergraduate I had been at Wayne State—the one who had compared so favorably to her University of Michigan beau because of the time he took to talk to her and the attention he showed through various small gifts. She longed for the young man who, while poor as a matchstick, had great generosity of spirit.

I couldn't understand what she meant, because I didn't really accept my failings. In my mind, I was responsible for the family, and I wanted to marshal every bit of my force and will to shape life's circumstances.

I did take time for the family too. When Michael turned eight, I began coaching his Little League team. For years, I rushed out of the office to coach the team (and later Laura's), and we made the seasons great times of family togetherness.

What did Nancy mean I wasn't the man she married? I was better—the ultimate provider and a great father. I never even played golf or hung around with my cronies. If I wasn't working,

I was with the family. I'd play a few sets of tennis, sure, but only once a week at most, in the evenings.

Despite my self-justifications and the evidence I could adduce in their support, Nancy knew not just that things weren't right, but also that *I* wasn't. In my heart of hearts, I knew that too. I wasn't willing to admit to it, though, and when Nancy began to see a counselor to deal with her frustrations, I refused to accompany her.

I never realized how truly depressed Nancy had become. I didn't have an inkling, for instance, that she spent long days calculating whether she'd be better off without me. She was that aggrieved at the changes in me, although she never admitted to the true depth of her suffering.

Fortunately, what Nancy couldn't say, one of my best friends did. Gene Driker and I came to know each other through working on the alumni board for Wayne State's law school. We also saw each other occasionally because he represented my partner and me in business dealings, and our families would sometimes socialize. Gene has a balanced, wise temperament and a profound capacity for empathy. He was among the very few in whom I felt I could confide.

He proved his friendship by telling me the uncomfortable truth in August of 1979. He wrote me an unforgettable letter that began, "I'm worried about you!" For some time, he had been concerned about the pace I was maintaining and its effect on Nancy. Previously, he had advised Nancy to seek counseling and had offered to make the necessary arrangements. He finally couldn't keep from confronting me directly, putting what he had to say in a letter to let me reflect on its contents.

Gene noted that I didn't look well—my eyes weren't clear. Either I looked exhausted or hyped up and nervous as a cat. "You are totally preoccupied with your work to an unhealthy extent," he wrote, and he cited times and places where he had observed these distress signals. He let me know that I was drinking "too damn much." I had to acknowledge that was the case. I couldn't relax anymore without alcohol.

Gene was kind enough to put all this in the context of his own experience. He knew the temptations to do just as I was doing. But he kept laying it on the line. "I think," he wrote, "you have allowed yourself to get trapped by your success — professional and financial — and if you're not careful, that success can ruin you." He noted the practical impossibility of my two full-time positions as a partner in S&G Investments and in the law firm. I had always prided myself on my stamina, my ability to work on little sleep and to grind my opponents down through sheer exertion.

"It's time to get over this brave front!" he continued. "You are kidding yourself if you think you can keep up this crazy pace without serious consequences to your physical and mental health, not to mention the impact on the family."

Gene advised me to get away — far away — with Nancy for a good, long period. However fine a lawyer I might be, if I dropped dead, my clients would mourn me one day and find another lawyer the next.

His letter closed with the words "I love you like a brother."

Gene's letter certainly got my attention, and I tried to employ its suggested remedies. Nancy and I took extended trips to London and Italy. We had wonderful times wandering the streets and dining in out-of-the-way restaurants and cafés. We also decided that our social life had become too frantic, and we cut back.

These "fixes" didn't really address the problem, though. Nancy enjoyed the trips overseas, but she still couldn't talk to me, because I was the same man in Rome that I was in Detroit. The Band-Aids we applied to our marriage provided comfort but no real healing. I was still as obsessed with work as ever, although I was beginning to crack under the pressure. I sometimes day-dreamed about having a heart attack—a mild one—so that I'd have a legitimate excuse for fending off work's demands.

One weekend Sonny and his wife and Nancy and I were invited to Florida by my brother's friend. In the wee hours of the morning, this friend clapped me on the back and said that Sonny and I were the two toughest men he had ever known.

I raised my glass and said, "Yes, and you'll never know how tough it is to be so tough." I took a drink as tears came down my cheeks.

□ □ □

When stagflation hit in the late 1970s and early 1980s, and commercial loan interest rates rose to 20 percent and higher, S&G Investments faced a major crisis. Our holding company bought businesses in various sectors to reduce risk—the same way a diversified portfolio of stocks works. All our holdings were highly leveraged, however, and the high interest rates were making it difficult to make any money. If one or more of our businesses suffered reversals, the layered structure we had built over the past five years could collapse. Our investors saw this and wanted to liquidate while there was still time.

Randy and I wanted to stay the course. Liquidation would return the principal plus some minor profits to our investors, but it would wipe out all the work that the two of us had devoted to developing the company's long-term value.

In 1981, Randy and I decided to buy out our partners, if we could find the financing. We were far from sure that anyone would loan us the money. Even if they did, the stratospheric interest rates might wipe us out.

We saw the potential of our businesses, though, and we were concerned about the ramifications for our employees if we decided to liquidate. I used to keep track of the number of people working in our companies on a sheet in my wallet. I remember how proud I was the day that figure passed three thousand. So there were many, many livelihoods at stake.

Still, I'm not sure I would ever have taken the risk if it weren't for the tremendous synergy Randy and I had as partners. We loved planning together, making the deals, and seeing the businesses we bought thrive. We had a particular knack for acquiring niche manufacturers that made very practical things like agricultural packaging machines, school bus seats, and auto parts. Our businesses helped make things run, which went straight to my long-held aspiration to be a builder of society. What I took to be my destiny was on the line.

Stern and Garb gave us ninety days to put together our financing. Our initial inquiries at the usual banks were spurned. We finally received a tentative commitment from GE Credit, which would supply the needed funding, but we had to move quickly.

I put everything I owned on the line as collateral, including our home—the house in which Nancy had grown up. Despite the shadows in our marriage, Nancy, while fearful, was willing to take the risk. I promised her that no matter what it took, we would never want for anything.

Mel Garb had a platonic crush on Nancy. He'd always make sure to remind me that I had married far above me. He called Nancy and told her, in a genuine way, that I was crazy to take the risk of the buyout, but if she ever needed anything, she could always depend on him. He actually called her for years thereafter to see how she was doing.

We just managed to get the closing documents together before the deadline we were given, and we had a grand signing session in Detroit that took most of the night. Randy and his wife, Judy, and Nancy and I went from one room to another in the lawyers' offices, posting our property as collateral here and taking on millions in debt there. It was heady stuff. At GE Credit's 23 percent interest rate, the monthly interest payments looked staggering.

We did have a workable strategy to handle the debt, all things being equal—which they almost never are in business. Several of our companies, including F&M Distributors and an auto parts maker called G&L, had begun to generate a lot of cash. The investment company also owned a string of Burger Kings in Southern California. As restaurants, these franchises were performing poorly, but the property they occupied had appreciated tremendously. We sold off the Burger Kings and their real estate and held on to the cash for debt servicing.

Interest rates were at record levels. If we could only hold out until they began to fall again, we'd win our enormous bet.

President Ronald Reagan had just come into office, and his slogan, "It's morning in America again," became fiscal reality within eighteen months of his election. The prime rate was at an astounding 20.5 percent on January 2, 1981. By October 13, 1982, it had fallen to 12 percent.

Despite living with great fear and uncertainty, Randy and I were able to refinance all our company's debt within one year. Buying out our business partners at economic midnight, during one of the darkest times the American economy has ever seen, we and the companies now in our possession woke up to the economic boom of the early Reagan years. We had made it.

□ □ □

By late 1982, at age forty-two, I had accomplished my primary career goals. I felt I was a real help to my law clients. I'd wanted to build an enterprise whose companies would manufacture useful goods and provide gainful employment. That dream had come true as well. Piling up wealth was never my motivation, but I had succeeded in providing financial security for my family.

Randy and I wanted to base our reborn company's name on one of America's great symbols, the eagle. We were grateful to the American system and the opportunities it afforded to people like us to become self-made men. We found that the eagle had been used too often in business names, so we settled for a representative part: the talons. In 1981, S&G Investments became Talon, Inc. We liked to joke that we had clawed our way to the top—that we had succeeded by getting others in our clutches. In truth, Talon was the product of smarts, hard work, free markets, and the friendship and trust Randy and I shared, all of which gave us the confidence to place a long bet on an economic recovery at the right time.

The public side of the Talon story was all to the good. Yet somehow, when I reflected on my success once the pressure eased, I didn't feel like jumping up and down. Gene's portrait of a work-obsessed, bleary-eyed man hurrying to the grave remained truer than ever. In fact, now that my wildest dreams had come true, life seemed to lose its savor entirely. Everything tasted like cardboard. Was this what I had been chasing after? Who had I become?

Chapter Five

The Turning Point

In the fall of 1983, Nancy and I received an invitation to a dinner being held at the Country Club of Detroit. Nancy was vague about the details, but she clearly wanted to go. I quizzed her: Who is giving the dinner?

She wasn't sure.

Was it a political fund-raiser?

"No," she said, "it's religious."

"Religious? Why would I go to a religious deal? I'm not going to change who I am or what I believe. You know that."

"That's not the point. Barb Voorheis said the dinner would be good for our marriage."

Barb was a close friend and someone I respected. Still, I said, "I thought we were going to cut down on social invitations. Can't we get out of it?"

I hoped Nancy would drop the matter and promptly forgot all about the invitation. As far as religion went, I believed my faith was better than most. I was proud to be a Catholic, the inheritor of twenty centuries of theological reflection, worship, and spiritual discipline inspired by the life and work of Christ. My faith had a true and certain meaning, and talk of a "religious" event outside of the Catholic Church made me deeply suspicious.

When I went to Mass each Sunday, however, I was conscious of a growing absence of feeling. I no longer felt close to God or even the people in my life. My life had become so filled with churning pressures that I seemed to be navigating through white-water rapids. I had to control everything at every moment, or life would spin totally out of control. There was something I needed more than my friend Gene's prescription of extended breaks.

Our son, Michael, had begun to rebel against me. In junior high, he had secluded himself in his room playing Dungeons & Dragons for hours, emerging only, it seemed, to lance his dragon father's heart with ever greater vehemence. When running back and forth from work to his Little League games, I'd congratulated myself on what an attentive and self-sacrificing father I was. I soon discovered that the only perfect parents are those whose children have yet to reach adolescence.

The damage to our relationship went further back than I ever could have imagined. Michael saw his mother suffering from my neglect for many years. He told Nancy to divorce me—the family would be better off without me. I was completely oblivious to this, and knowing of it now I can only shake my head and stifle the tears. I had been thinking of the outward things, not what was going on in my young son's heart, which I had no means of fathoming.

Mike and Laura attended a wonderful private school, Grosse Pointe Academy, through their elementary and middle school years. It had once been run by Sacred Heart sisters and had subsequently been taken over by the laity. Still, the school had a distinctive Christian emphasis. Provision was made for the Catholic children to receive instruction in preparation for First Communion and Confirmation. Nancy and I alternated serving on the board there, and I was for a time head of development. In this respect we were involved parents.

We had a close enough sense of our community to know how affluence was undermining traditional values. The drug culture was rampant. As Michael prepared to go into high school, Nancy decided he needed a broader view of life and more discipline than the local high school might provide. We decided to send him to U of D High, my alma mater, where he'd receive more of a classical education and get to know classmates from the inner city.

At first Michael wanted no part of a Catholic high school. But I believed in the "golden rule": He who has the gold rules. I sat Michael down and told him that I was going to give him ten good reasons why he should attend U of D High. If he could give me ten good reasons why he shouldn't, we'd discuss it. Naturally, he couldn't. I told him to try it for a year, and then if he still had objections, we'd talk about them once more.

Michael began to enjoy U of D High, but he was still rebellious. For instance, he and a friend were caught with a small amount of marijuana on a religious retreat. I had to plead with the president for him not to be expelled, invoking the family's history at the school and promising we'd seek counseling for Michael. The kind man went out on a limb and granted my request.

Despite the Band-Aids Nancy and I had applied to our marriage—the pleasant trips we had taken together—we were still no closer. As I dealt, even to a limited degree, with her unhappiness, I became uncomfortably aware of my indifference to her. I still loved her profoundly in the sense of maintaining my absolute commitment to her, but I had to acknowledge that she didn't inspire many loving feelings. As our marriage became more and more distant, our relationship became just one more problem I had to manage.

So I'd go to church and pray to feel something, anything. I realized that I was dying inside. I asked God to deliver me from this death, over and over.

My frustration with my spiritual condition resulted in a hyper-critical attitude toward my parish. On the way home from Mass, I'd tell Nancy things like, "That was such a lousy sermon."

I didn't think the problem could be with me—not in any big way. What sin was I guilty of? I didn't commit adultery. I went to Mass weekly, went to confession periodically, and supported the parish and other Catholic ministries with my offerings. If I drank to excess on occasion and was known to pound the table and turn the air blue at business meetings, that was just being a man. No one could do what I did without becoming upset. People couldn't be counted on to get the message unless you showed them what was at stake. I overworked, true, but my family reaped the benefits. Whatever suffering my work habits caused came first out of my own hide.

Yet each Sunday, as I went forward to take Communion, I would beg God to help me feel His presence even as I felt myself moving further and further away from Him.

Often I'd lie awake at night asking myself why in the world I couldn't be happy. I had become a success after all. I had everything I'd always wanted. Randy enjoyed his wealth and the big-boy toys it allowed him to buy. He knew how to play and enjoy himself, but I couldn't even enjoy the money. I couldn't escape the terrible knowledge that like so many of the wealthy clients I represented, my personal life was a shambles.

I hardly breathed a word of this to anyone, of course. I did make one confession to a close friend of mine, a lawyer named John. We were at a men's fund-raiser for a hospital, and we were drinking together. "John, I can hardly stand how I'm living," I said. "Nothing is worth it. I just feel so lousy. Sometimes I get so down, I feel like I could end it all. Really."

He said, "You know, Mike, I understand exactly how you feel. I just read this book called *Born Again* by Chuck Colson, and I'm going to bring it over to you."

The next day he brought me the book. He'd written a letter to me, in which he expressed once more that he understood my feelings and that maybe this book would help. I put the book with its yellow and black cover on my nightstand and left it there for years before finally reading it.

The only comfort I did obtain during this time of despair came through my daughter, Laura. I was crazy about her. She was very spunky and tried hard at everything. She was principally her mother's girl, and that made me try all the harder to win her affection. She reciprocated mostly by teasing, which I loved.

By this time in Laura's life, age thirteen, she was tall, very bright, and looked far older than she was. A lefty, she played a mean game of tennis and was popular with everyone. She could get cheeky at times, but she was not truly rebellious and unhappy like Michael.

During the previous several years, I'd made it a habit to take her on father-daughter trips. I took her for weekends on the town in Chicago and New York, and we had tremendous times together. She was very expressive, both talkative and an active writer. When Nancy and I would go out, she'd leave notes for us by our bedside; usually a thank-you for a present we'd given her or a special permission.

Many nights when I'd return home late from work, I'd climb the stairs and stop off in her bedroom. I would sit by her bed, and I would kiss her cheek and smell that special child smell. I'd sit on the floor next to her bed and thank God for her because she was such a gift to us. Watching over Laura as she slept gave me a strange kind of peace.

□ □ □

I have no memory of speaking with Nancy again about the "religious" event at the country club until we were headed out the door to attend. I suppose I went along because it was something she thought would improve our marriage, but I can't even say that for certain. I still didn't want to be there, and I was in a foul mood upon arrival.

A friend greeted me near the door, and in a teasing way asked the relevant question: "Mike, what the hell are you doing here?"

"Probably what you are," I said. "Making my wife happy."

"Let's go down to the bar and have a See-Through," he said. "These things never start on time."

I never drank martinis, so I said I'd better not. Nancy and I were on difficult enough terms already.

Nancy and I walked over to our table in the country club's central hall, with its high, arched ceiling, huge, round, wooden chandeliers, and gray stone walls. It looked like a castle's banquet room. I noticed as I passed other tables that women were chatting with one another happily while the men looked away, shifting their eyes to avoid those of their peers, I assumed.

My unease was compounded when a fellow lawyer took his place next to us. His greeting was hesitant, and his quick, nervous questions seemed aimed at taking my temperature. He was in my black book because he was poaching on one of my clients. We wouldn't have a lot to talk about that evening.

Mercifully, the program started shortly after dinner was served. The headliners for the evening were a PGA tour player, Rik Massengale, and his wife, Cindy. They would speak about the problems in their marriage that resulted from Rik's obsession with his career.

But first, Bob Orr, a local man and an accountant with Ford, gave a talk. His presentation was unpretentious and obviously genuine. "I don't know why they asked me to speak tonight," he said. "I've never done it before. But I'll tell you a very simple story. All my life I've had this tremendous hunger to know God personally, and one Friday night while I was working on my sailing gear, I knelt down by my workbench, and I asked Jesus to come into my life and make me the kind of man He wants me to be."

What Bob said shocked me for a number of reasons. I admire guts; it certainly took tremendous courage to stand before 250 of his neighbors and talk so openly about Jesus. I'd never heard a layperson speak that way before. The simplicity in how he committed his life to Jesus got my attention as well. Sailing is a big deal in Grosse Pointe. Many people own boats and spend all their free time either planning or going on outings or working on their gear in the winter. So we could all relate to the scene—a very acceptable country-club topic. But there was Bob, telling us that in the midst of living a life like ours—a good life—he found himself longing to know God. And I could see in his face that God had answered his prayer. He had found something that I didn't have—real joy in living.

Bob's wish to know God resonated deeply with my own prayers before the altar. I wanted God to deliver me from my life's loss of meaning and the depression that went with it.

So as Rik and Cindy Massengale spoke, telling a similar story about how their conversions turned their lives around and healed their marriage, I kept thinking about what Bob had said.

At the end of the evening, the emcee led those who wanted to know God in the way that Bob and the Massengales did in a prayer of commitment. I remember thinking that these people had a lot of courage, getting up in front of an audience and sharing intimate details about their life—but, most importantly, talking about Jesus. I knew they had something I didn't have, and I wanted desperately to feel the way they did.

I said the prayer. I confessed that I was a sinner, that Christ had died for my sins, and asked Jesus to be my Savior and my Lord.

After the prayer, the event organizers turned our attention to the information cards on the table. They asked those of us who had prayed the prayer of commitment to fill out a card; they'd be sending us follow-up materials about living as a follower of Jesus. Without anyone seeing me, I filled out a card.

That night at the Country Club of Detroit, November 10, 1983, I wasn't thinking about the world of things my prayer of commitment might imply. I wasn't thinking about my Catholic upbringing or my life as a lawyer and businessman. I didn't need to inquire too closely into the brand of Christianity being represented at the dinner either. I felt moved to pray—to reach out to God as Bob had once done—and so I did, sincerely and with all my heart. I knew I was dying inside, and I wanted to live.

As Nancy and I drove home that evening, we didn't speak directly about how the evening affected us. We may have commented in passing that this "religious" dinner hadn't turned out to be too kooky. I didn't feel any bells or whistles going off in me, but I had a quiet understanding that I had done something pleasing to God. If someone had told me that I had just experienced the turning point of my entire life, I wouldn't have understood that. I often prayed, and I certainly didn't see the far-reaching consequences of my prayer. But from that moment on, I can see now, I began to live again.

If I had known that Nancy had also said the prayer and signed a follow-up card, I might have been more intrigued about what the evening would eventually come to mean in our lives. But I wouldn't know of Nancy's commitment for weeks.

Chapter Six

Going Deeper, Moving Outward

While I felt that God was pleased with my prayer of commitment, I had no expectations of future consequences. I mean that—none. I suppose I hoped the peace in my spirit that night would endure, at least for a time. Otherwise I expected life to go on as before. That I would be growing into a whole new life was the last thing on my mind.

About a week after the Country Club of Detroit dinner, I received a phone call from a man named Jim. He quickly told me that he attended our Catholic parish, St. Paul's, and that he was associated with the organizing group for the dinner at the country club. He said this in a rush, as if he couldn't quite catch his breath.

"Would you like to come to a men's Bible study?" he asked.

"No," I replied.

"But . . . remember . . . the cards?" he said. "We said we'd get back to you with more information. The Bible study is one way of doing that."

"What are the other ways?" I asked, not letting him off the hook.

"If you could come just once. . . . It's really a tremendous group of men."

I had done enough fund-raising for political campaigns, school projects, and community events to know how ill at ease this was making him.

"Did you draw the short end of the stick and have to call me?" I asked.

At that, his voice began to break.

So I said, "All right, I'll come, just once because you had the courage to call me, and I know what that's like."

The meeting was in downtown Detroit at the Renaissance Club. On the drive there, I was fighting with myself. I told myself this was stupid, that I was going to be embarrassed, that I would have nothing in common with the bunch of holy rollers I was sure would be there.

I had given my word, though, and I kept it.

A man named Dick Robarts led the study. He drove through the tunnel every week from Windsor, Ontario, and I respected his effort. He possessed a wide-ranging knowledge of the Bible, jumping from the Old to the New Testament.

Impressed as I was with Dick's teaching, I also admired the demeanor of the fifteen or so men who sat around a long conference table. They were friendly without being over-eager. They took what was being discussed seriously without any hand-pressed piety. The discussion of the text was much like a group of lawyers considering a point of law. Each man had a Bible with him, except me.

When the meeting ended with a time of collective prayer, many prayed aloud, easily and naturally. They voiced the challenges in their lives. There was nothing showy or embarrassingly personal in these petitions. These men were simply talking to God, with due restraint because of the public forum and yet with an unmistakable authenticity. They neither hid nor flaunted their spirituality. It was real. I had not said one word during the entire discussion, which was some kind of miracle.

The next week, I drove downtown eagerly and with a Bible of my own. Once I became comfortable at the Bible study, I started speaking up. The others admitted they thought they'd never see me again after my first stony visit.

Studying the Bible was as promised, a revelation. As a lifelong Catholic who had been educated in Catholic schools through twelfth grade, I knew much of the Scripture's content. But I knew considerably less than I had imagined about the Bible's structure — its overarching story. Catholics read the Bible every single Sunday, a section from the Old Testament, a psalm, another reading from the Epistles, and a selection from the Gospels. Similarly, there are three readings at daily Mass. The Scripture readings at Mass are meant to be touchstones for the ministry of the Word — the preaching. They are short nuggets of Scripture — in technical terms, pericopes.

Reading the Scriptures in this way is a great spur to preaching and meditation. Unfortunately, it has shortcomings when it comes to the Bible's big picture and its worldview consequences. What if you read a mystery story like that, with a small sample from the first chapters, another from the middle, and one from the end? You'd eventually know a lot about the book, but it might remain difficult to understand the central mystery. You'd keep forgetting the various characters and their function, and while some plot points would stick in your mind, others would get lost. That's why many faithful Catholics say they "don't know the Bible," when they read it at least every Sunday.[2]

As I began to read the Bible in a different way, great chunks of it at a time and straight through one book after another in consecutive order, I found myself jolted by the magnificent story the whole Bible tells. God creates us so that we can enjoy His love and friendship and the world of wonder and awe in which He places us. We rebel, thinking we can usurp God's place, which leaves men and women alienated from the One to whom we owe our very existence, God Himself. Yet God, like a spurned yet hopeful lover, continues to draw us back to Him, first through His relationship with and the promises He made to Abraham, which were codified in the law given to Moses.

If you had put all these statements to me before I began studying the Bible intensely, I would have agreed with them. There's nothing different here from what I had always been taught. And yet, when the Scriptures became my "food and drink," when they began to infuse my thoughts and direct my actions, my belief in Christ and the presence of the Spirit became real in an entirely new way. The Bible came to life for me.

I enjoyed making connections among the Bible's multiple story lines—for example, how David's life anticipates the Savior who was to come—and considering how one passage comments on another. Dick took me under his wing, and we went through Bible study materials from the evangelical organization Campus Crusade for Christ. Dick's tutoring was a tremendous help.

In the next months, I suppose I transferred some of my workaholism into Christaholism, as I began studying Scripture for as many as six to eight hours a day. I couldn't get enough of it. I began to realize that I couldn't just have my faith as one has a possession like a car or a fine suit. God wanted to love me. I had to choose whether to love Him back in every action of my life, big and small. I had to face whether Jesus was the Lord of my life or I was in charge.

Soon I realized this was a process that would continue throughout my life. Whenever I found that I was putting my own ego back in charge, I had to stop, think again, and submit every aspect of my life as a "living sacrifice" to God. In this way, God could direct me to what He alone knew to be the ends for which I was made—in this life and the one to come.

Once I started not merely reading the Bible but studying it, I couldn't believe I had never done it before. And one day I came to a realization that put it into a legal-business context for me: The Bible was a contract between God and the Jews in the Old Testament, and whenever they kept the terms of the contract, they prospered; when they violated the terms, they suffered. Jesus came to extend that contract to all men and women, as He said in the New Testament. And like any contract, there is an offer and an acceptance. The offer is eternal life and peace on this earth if I accept Jesus Christ as my Lord and Savior and attempt to live by His teachings. I realized that I had entered into a contract with God—a contract that He would fulfill, even if I failed at some of the contract's provisions.

The first effect of my Bible study was a renewal of my joy in life—in every part of life, not merely those aspects we think of as religious. I hadn't been this excited about living for a very long time. I knew Jesus was alive and working in me, answering the prayer I'd prayed at the country club.

I wondered, of course, why we didn't have these types of Bible studies in the Catholic Church, at least to my knowledge.[3] I wanted to know what the Church's official position was about lay Catholics reading the Bible, so I read the relevant Vatican II document, *Dei Verbum* (Dogmatic Constitution on Divine Revelation). I found that the Church urged all Catholics to immerse themselves in the Scriptures. The Church "forcefully and specifically exhorts all the Christian faithful . . . to learn 'the surpassing knowledge of Jesus Christ' (Phil. 3:8) by frequent reading of the divine Scriptures."[4]

Dei Verbum points out the transforming effect of Bible study as well.

> Such is the force and power of the Word of God that it can serve . . . the children of the Church as strength for their faith, food for the soul, and a pure and lasting fount of spiritual life. Scripture verifies in the most perfect way the words: "The word of God is living and active" (Heb. 4:12), and "is able to build you up and to give you the inheritance among all those who are sanctified" (Acts 20:32; cf. 1 Th. 2:13).

I had corroborated in my own experience the document's assertion: "This nourishment [the Divine Word] enlightens the mind, strengthens the will and fires the hearts of men with the love of God." The document is so strong on the importance of Bible study that it repeats the warning of St. Jerome that has resonated down the ages: "Ignorance of the Scriptures is ignorance of Christ."[5]

Why hadn't I known of the Church's position before? Why wasn't it being taught and Bible studies implemented by every parish? I realized that, in my enthusiasm for the gifts of evangelicalism, I shouldn't presume neglect of these gifts by the Catholic Church. There did seem to be a disconnect between the official position of the Church and the practice of many parishes in this regard, but that didn't mean that the Church's teaching was flawed so much as its day-to-day practice.

I began to feel that God was directing me to reach out to my fellow Catholics and in doing so to be active, faithful, and supportive rather than critical. I began going to daily Mass to set an example, but in a very short time I realized that God was using this to draw me closer and closer to Him. Nancy and I determined that we would always use a portion of our time, talent, and resources for Catholic evangelism.

□ □ □

During this time of awakening for me, I sensed God's urging to make additional changes in my life. These would prove increasingly rewarding, if more and more difficult.

I first came into a deeper understanding of repentance, fittingly enough, while enjoying a cigarette and a stiff drink. In February 1984, on a wintry Sunday afternoon, I was reading through the book of Ephesians. I had a fire going and my feet up as I was smoking a cigarette and sipping a Perfect Manhattan. The drink's combination of sweet and dry vermouth and whiskey tasted just right.

In the midst of this pleasant interlude, I heard a still, small voice. In a friendly way, the voice asked a simple question: "Why are you smoking and drinking?"

"To relax," I responded.

"Why don't you learn to relax in Me?" Jesus seemed to be saying.

Was that possible?

I stubbed out my cigarette and poured my drink down the drain. I hadn't made any resolutions exactly, although as it happened I would never smoke again. I was simply willing to see whether reading the Bible alone could quell my restlessness.

Is mine just the old fundamentalist story of dos and don'ts? The smoking and drinking themselves weren't big things. You have to see how Jesus was inviting me into what His presence alone confers—real peace. Not long before, my life had been a furious contest with what I've described as the "rapids." The Lord was trying to show me that my life was a white-water ride of my own devising. I had lost the ability to turn the turbulence off, but given the opportunity, He could do so in a moment. Reading the Scriptures calmed me down, turned off the crashing of the waves around me, and made the liquor unnecessary. Jesus called out over the stormy waters, "Peace, be still."

As I continued to study, the Scriptures became a mirror in which I could see myself ever more clearly. The more I looked into the Bible, the less I liked my reflection. I had convinced myself that I didn't sin, apart from a few minor diversions that seemed the right of every red-blooded American male. I considered my own virtue far superior to others'. After all, I had never cheated on my wife. I knew many men who had, of course, and I avoided doing business with them, reasoning that if a man couldn't keep his marital vows, then how could he be relied upon in a business situation?

A friend would later point out that I had cheated on my wife every single day by making work the be-all and end-all of my existence. In his view, my sin was worse than that of a man who's unable to resist sexual temptation—a sin of mere human weakness. I had made a choice, and in reality the choice was me and my career.

When I began making Jesus the Lord of my life, I saw immediately that what I took to be excusable diversions—drinking, swearing, telling dirty jokes, and the like—were symptoms of a serious underlying spiritual condition: pride. I thought I should be able to control everything and everyone around me, and when I couldn't, I felt compelled to divert myself. My self-righteous attitude only confirmed how imprisoned I was in pride's "castle in the air."

I took immediate steps to address the problem that was

uppermost in my mind: Nancy's unhappiness and my coolness toward her. Soon after I had begun attending my downtown men's group, Nancy had informed me that she had said a prayer of commitment as well. How glad I was that she and I would be growing in the Lord together! I changed my schedule so that we could have more time to talk.

In the first weeks of my spiritual renewal, I started attending Mass every morning. Then, before heading to the office, I'd come home and have a cup of coffee with Nancy, usually in the seating area in our bedroom. She had often remarked that we'd have a happy marriage if only we spent our lives in the car. "You actually talk to me when we're in the car," she'd say. So I tried to devote the best hour in my day, the time when I'm mentally sharpest, to talking with and listening to Nancy.

She appreciated this, but things didn't go quite as swimmingly as I'd imagined. After we had kept our coffee hour together for a short time, I made a cardinal mistake for a lawyer. I asked a leading question to which I didn't know the answer. I said, "Honey, look at us, don't you think we're communicating better?"

"No, not at all," she said and burst into tears.

On the way into the office, I had a long and heated talk with the Lord. "What's going on?" I asked Him. "I'm really trying. I'm giving Nancy the best hour in my day. I bite my tongue so she won't accuse me of being argumentative. I'm doing my level best. Are you hearing me, Lord?"

Relax, God seemed to say, *you're making progress. Just keep going.*

Our mutual commitment to the Lord slowly began to draw us closer once more. The activities in Christ we started engaging in, like outreach dinners, brought a new solidarity to our marriage. As we began working for God's kingdom together, Nancy began to see, once more, the Mike Timmis who could be generous in his love. I saw the gracious lady who could tell the difference between my better self and my successful persona, and who loved the only thing that's truly lovable about anyone—the image of God within. The love I had once felt for Nancy from moment to moment rushed back in. We were like two kids reuniting after a long separation on different continents.

□ □ □

I also felt an obligation to relate differently to my business colleagues to eliminate the element of fear I had conveyed to them. I cut out the swearing and throwing temper tantrums in meetings. I also had a series of one-on-one chats with colleagues, and I told them I wanted to make sure everything we did at the law firm and in the business was beyond reproach. Not only were we not going to cross the line, we weren't going to get close. I apologized if anything I had said in the past had created a different impression.

I also started telling people what had happened to me—that I had committed my life to Jesus as never before. Of course I worried about how Randy would react. As it turned out, he was delighted for me and had no problem with any changes my renewed faith dictated in the way we did business.

One incident in particular confirmed how he supported me in business ethics. Talon had acquired a shopping center, and we were having trouble filling the space. Randy and I were talking to the president of our real estate operations about this. The president excused the shopping center's poor performance on the basis of restrictions I had imposed. Randy asked what he meant. "I could have put a big video store in," the man replied, "but Mike said we couldn't rent to them because they carried X-rated films."

He looked at Randy, raised his eyebrows, and cocked his head in my direction. "You know Mike."

Randy would have none of this. "If that's the way Mike wants it, then that's the way it will be." End of discussion.

Once I had put some disagreeable habits aside by the aid of God's grace, I looked more deeply into why anger and its shadow, impatience, kept besetting me. I found that just beneath the surface I was extremely angry. I was carrying residual rage. When my mother died, I had hardened myself to make my own way no matter what. I had put myself under so much pressure to that end that my spirit had gone from fiery to molten. I needed God to cool my fevered soul. That would take time and involve, paradoxically, being placed in God's own crucible, which mercifully was still a ways off. (Admittedly, I still can be impatient. Short of heaven, working out one's salvation is a long road.)

As I studied with Dick and grew close to the men in the Bible study, I began to adopt evangelical Christian ways. I had been living in such despair and now, feeling as joyful in my faith as I had once as a child, I really did feel reborn, or "born again." This was the greatest thing that had ever happened to me. I became what my friends call an evangelical Catholic, and in those days the emphasis was definitely on the evangelical side.

When you think about it, all Christians are evangelicals; it's simply the nature of the gospel message. The Great Commission to go into all nations and preach the gospel applies to every follower of Jesus.

Naturally, I wanted to tell people about how I had been delivered from a living death — how I had been born again. I had found the cure for eternal cancer! My evangelical friends introduced me to Campus Crusade's *Four Spiritual Laws* and The Navigators' *Steps to Peace with God*, booklets that summarize how to become a committed Christian. I used these everywhere—on planes, on trains, and in automobiles, in hospitals, with neighbors, and at lunches with colleagues and associates.

A lot of people were receptive—even taxi drivers. You'd be surprised how many folks never have anyone ask them about their spiritual commitments or anything they truly care about. I verified for myself Thoreau's line: "The mass of men lead lives of quiet desperation." Within a few months of my reawakening, I saw more than a few accept Jesus as their Savior and Lord.

Sometimes people showed little interest, but I didn't back off easily. I reasoned that the cure for eternal cancer might seem as unpleasant as chemotherapy—but since it worked, I wanted them to have it! I mean, I was ready to go out on the street corners, onto the highways and byways, and proclaim the gospel. I was, as my new evangelical friends liked to say, "totally sold out" to God.

I'll never forget two of my early experiences witnessing, in which I spoke with women dying of cancer. One was Janice, the secretary of my law partner. When I visited her in the hospital, she was extremely ill. Driving downtown to see her, I debated the wisdom of what I was doing. I felt the Lord was calling me to Janice's bedside, but what right did I have? I kept hearing a voice saying, "You have no right to do this. You have no right." I realize now that I was in the midst of spiritual warfare. God wanted me to go; the Devil didn't.

I told Janice of my experience with Jesus and that she could be assured of living with God if she gave herself into His care. As I was speaking, her parents walked in. This made continuing the conversation awkward, but I realized I shouldn't stop for the sake of pleasantries. Her parents gave Janice and me the moments we needed to finish our discussion.

We prayed together and Janice asked Christ into her life. I

could see how much she wanted to be with God. Later I went down to the waiting room and spoke with her parents, who didn't know me, and explained who I was and why I was there. They knew their daughter was dying and thanked me for my visit.

Janice passed away within twenty-four hours. In retrospect, I realized I had every right and responsibility to speak with her. That's why God had prompted me. In times of spiritual struggle, I needed to call on the Lord for His courage. This event made me bolder about acting on God's direction. His leading had presented a strange, somehow daunting task, and yet this task, like every calling from God, was in reality a gift. What if I had missed receiving it?

Later on, I spoke with another cancer victim. She was in her seventies, from Texas, and a very close friend. Everyone called her Sitty. By that time I had begun giving my testimony at public events, and I thought the best way to present my testimony to Sitty might be to play her a tape. So I carried a tape recorder to her home and asked if she'd listen.

When the tape finished, she asked, "Why have I never heard this before? I've gone to church all my life, but I've never heard this." Her question drove home the tragedy that some people with open hearts never hear the gospel. Her next question filled me with joy: "Mike, how do I ask Jesus into my life?"

□ □ □

My new commitment to faith upset my teenage son. Like my evangelical friends, I started carrying my Bible everywhere. This embarrassed Michael. He could see that I was changing, but he wasn't necessarily happy about it. I was suddenly interested in spending much more time with the family, but this upset the family's power structure. Michael was used to being second in command to his mom, at least in his mind. Now, as I became more active within the home, he felt his prestige and power within the family diminish; he was confined to the role of a child rather than a surrogate adult.

Michael had also accommodated my past absence by idealizing his father as a tough-as-nails powerhouse. He had bought into my public image. He saw me as an entrepreneurial wild man. For instance, Michael tells the story of how I came home from an office party that we gave in conjunction with the Detroit Grand Prix. Our guests could watch the race from an office building we had purchased, while enjoying a full bar and buffet. After the race, we held a poker game. That year I was the big winner. When I got home, still half lit-up, I found Michael and his friends in the basement, playing pool. I took the wad of cash I'd won and stuffed bills in my shirt and trouser pockets and cuffs, and then I hopped up on the pool table and did a celebratory jig. That was Michael's preferred image of his father.

Michael didn't feel particularly close to this wild-man father, but he persuaded himself that toughness, power, and cunning were admirable. His old man was someone to be reckoned with, even if he felt the need to keep me at arm's distance.

Now I was asking the family to do super-pious things like sit down on Sunday afternoons while I read the Bible to them. Nancy went along, quelling protests from Michael and Laura, whose expressions clearly said, "Are you serious? Do we have to do this?"

There were occasions when Michael could see that his new father proved far superior to the old one. We were on vacation in Florida, and I asked Michael to take the bags from our hotel room out to the car. I tossed him the car keys so that he could open the trunk. He did as he was asked, but when he finished, he realized that he had inadvertently locked the keys in the trunk along with the bags. He told me afterward that he expected an explosion from the terrible Timmis temper.

When I found out what he had done, and that Nancy didn't have a backup set of keys, I'm sure my blood pressure went through the roof, but I did not yell. I simply asked Nancy to call a locksmith while I took long, long breaths. This said a lot to Michael, who told me that's when he began to believe that something truly positive had happened in my life.

The two people in the world I most wanted to share Christ with were, of course, my kids. Even after seeing the changes in me, Michael remained wary. I constantly struck up conversations with him and began arguing the reasonableness of my beliefs.

"Dad, you're lawyering me," Michael would say.

Still, I didn't stop. One morning, in his senior year of high school, Michael was in the bathroom shaving. I saw him there and struck up another conversation with a spiritual intent.

"Dad," he finally asked me in exasperation, "how long was it until you found Jesus?"

"Forty-three years," I said.

"Well, I'm only eighteen," he said.

Even I had to laugh.

□ □ □

My concern for my family and a sense of how much I needed the support of other believers prompted me to ask two lifetime friends, Jim and Jesse, to meet with me. They naturally wanted to know what we would be discussing. "I'd like to start praying for our families," I told them. "Maybe we could read some Scripture together too."

That was in 1984. Thus began a study and accountability group that continues to this day. We meet, pray, read Scripture, discuss what's going on in our lives, and give each other our best advice. In a group like this, particularly one that endures for so long, you can hear what people are trying to tell you, even when their reflections hurt, because you know that what they say comes out of love.

Many of my other friends, particularly more casual acquaintances through business or neighborhood ties, were baffled by what had happened to me. They thought I had become a nut case and probably only continued associating with me because of my position in the community. I remember some saying, genuinely trying to be helpful, "Mike, why do you need this? You've always been a good man."

At that point, I had learned enough to confess, "No, I wasn't a good man. I just thought I was a good man, but I was kidding myself."

□ □ □

After about a year of studying with Dick, I was asked to tell my story of spiritual reawakening at another evangelistic dinner at the Country Club of Detroit. By this time, I understood that my first watershed dinner and the men's Bible study had been organized by the Executive Ministries division of Campus Crusade for Christ. I would soon meet the founder of the organization, Bill Bright, and key players in Executive Ministries, particularly Nancy DeMoss, who was from Philadelphia.

Dick and I went over and over each line of what I was going to say. He impressed on me that since I would be representing

Christ, every word and gesture had to be weighed and measured. I was just as eager to honor my Lord, who had "turned my mourning into gladness."

My wife and I invited as many of our Catholic friends to attend as possible. We followed up on the written invitations with phone calls to those we thought might be receptive.

I had read enough Scripture by this time to know that a prophet is without honor in his own country. I was planning to get up in front of my friends and draw a line in the temporal sand. People knew the old Mike Timmis, and now I was speaking of the new creature I was in Christ. I felt the pressure of my neighbors' natural skepticism and of future expectations. Even with God's grace, would I be able to maintain the new life I was proclaiming? What if I succumbed to temptations and discredited God's power through hypocrisy?

As everyone sat down to dinner, I was more than a little nervous. When it was my time to speak, I had my written remarks in front of me, and I'm sure I made the mistake of most neophyte speakers, sticking too closely to the page, losing contact with my audience. Still, this was a huge occasion for me. A peer can sometimes reach those who would never listen to a priest or a minister. I sweated the speech the whole way through.

At the end of the evening, the emcee commented on his own story — how he had been married twice and then met his present wife at a Bible study. This was hanging one's linen out to dry in a way that made me cringe.

I started whispering feverishly to Nancy, "Why's he doing that when we've brought all our Catholic friends here? If I'd have heard that the first time, I would have walked out!"

"Michael," she said, "he said exactly the same thing the first time."

"No, he didn't."

"Yes, he did," she said. "He's giving his prepared thoughts just like everybody else."

I realized she was right. I also realized that the Lord had prevented me from hearing what he had said that first night. Since then I've always prayed that if I say publicly anything that someone's not ready to hear, the Lord will do the same for that person. This incident also taught me a lesson about being judgmental. The moderator had become a genuine and loving follower of Jesus, so who was I to judge him?

I don't recall much about the end of that evening other than feeling exhausted. I think many of my neighbors remained mystified, believing that I had fallen under the influence of a cult.

The evangelical Christians in the audience were enthusiastic, of course. If I hadn't known it before, I understood that night how much Executive Ministries and similar efforts depend on what might be called "trophy converts." At least in terms of the Detroit community, I had position, wealth, and status. If Mike Timmis felt there was something to this born-again business, well then, maybe it merited a look. I suppose many people do reason in this way, and that's what gives trophy converts their usefulness. There are many dangers to this approach, though, and even as I took my first spin around the speaking circuit, giving my testimony again and again in the coming months, I sensed them.

At the same time, I learned a lot through giving my testimony in public, particularly in terms of discerning what is in people's hearts. Nancy DeMoss, the wonderful woman behind Executive Ministries, asked me to come to New York and speak at a dinner in Manhattan. She asked if I'd like to invite anyone I knew in the city. At the time, my firm was doing some work on Wall Street, and I had come to know a high-ranking partner at the investment firm Goldman Sachs. I sent him an invitation.

When he walked through the door, I was immediately sorry I'd invited him. I felt embarrassed and presumed he would think I was a twit. But, of course, I got up and spoke anyway.

At the end of the evening, this man and his wife came up to me with tears in their eyes. They said, "We didn't know what to expect, but we are so grateful you invited us here."

I felt so ashamed for my earlier fears. From that moment I have never retreated—no matter how strong my inhibitions—from talking to someone about Jesus. After all, I'm not the one on the line, God is. And if God doesn't mind using me to speak of His reality, how can I possibly be ashamed of my experience in Him? I have asked forgiveness many, many times over for my initial embarrassment.

On another occasion, I was speaking to about 250 people in Morristown, New Jersey, at a Sunday brunch. The sister of a best friend lived in the area, and I invited her and her husband. When they walked through the door, they looked like deer caught in the headlights. They were "cradle Catholics" and had never been to an evangelical-sponsored event, where they were greeted enthusiastically by strangers in the name of religion. This was utterly foreign to them. I seated them next to me at our table, which was right by the podium.

As I gave my testimony, I became emotional and looked over at my table. The husband was weeping.

When I finished my talk and stepped away from the podium, this guy jumped up, wrapped his arms around me, and said for all to hear, "Mike, that was [expletive] beautiful!" The milling crowd immediately turned its attention to us, and the man realized what he had said. Still embracing me, he leaned back and spluttered, "Uh-oh, I didn't offend you, did I?"

"No," I said. "But let's just sit down now and talk about it."

A little later, another friend came up to me and said, "I'll give you a thousand dollars if you'll call Bill Bright and tell him what just happened."

At another speaking event in Greenville, South Carolina, I had a hard time getting through my talk, stumbling a bit with my words. Nevertheless, through the power of the Holy Spirit, my testimony had a tremendous impact. Those who wanted to talk with me afterward were invited to do so, and about forty people lined up. I was overwhelmed by the response.

A businessman was first in line. I was ready for him to ask me just about anything—or so I thought.

"May I ask you a personal question?" he said.

I had just spoken very candidly about my life and presumed there was little left to tell. I assured him he could ask me anything he wished.

"What do you think of Northwest Industries?" he asked.

"What do you mean, what do I think of Northwest Industries?"

"Well, you know of the company, don't you?" he continued. "Do you think it's going anywhere? Do you think it's a buy?"

I laughed and said, "I'm not a stockbroker," and I thanked him for coming.

After I greeted everyone in line, this businessman came up to me once more. "I'm still wondering what you think of Northwest Industries," he insisted. "Have you given it any more thought?"

The Lord finally opened my mind to this man's true desire. He wanted to connect with my story, but he didn't know how to start a spiritual conversation. He was reaching out in the only way he felt comfortable, by talking about business. "Northwest Industries is beyond me," I said, "but what did you think about my presentation?"

After that, we had a great talk about what it means to follow

Jesus. Through this and similar incidents, I learned to respond to where people are and how stray questions often conceal much deeper ones.

I also learned to rely on wisdom much greater than my own. As I engaged with people in a prayerful spirit, I found myself responding to them in ways that I couldn't have anticipated. Once I was scheduled to speak at a dinner in Porto, Portugal, which, as is the custom, began late in the evening, around eleven o'clock. We were served a white wine course and a red wine course and the city's eponymous port with dessert. I wondered whether anyone would care about what I had to say after that much wine.

Yet my testimony seemed to go well, and people once again wanted to talk with me afterward. A beautiful, petite, older woman greeted me. She wanted me to know that what I had said was fine, but she had her own way of praying. Her need to distinguish her own faith from mine and the self-contented way she presented herself told me, I guess, that she was not as confident of being in God's company as she wanted to appear.

I asked her how she knew she was praying to God and not to herself. "Before I gave my life completely to Jesus," I said, "I prayed a lot, but I was praying more to myself than to God."

Her confident expression broke apart as if I had just smashed a mirror.

"There's a way you can know whether you are praying to yourself or to God," I explained. "Go home and read the gospel of John. Then ask the Lord whether you are praying to Him or to yourself."

She went away, looking thoughtful.

When I had finished speaking with everyone in line, this elegant woman, now with her even more elderly chauffeur in tow, appeared before me again. It was now past two o'clock in the morning. "Tell my driver what you told me," she said. "I want him to hear it. I'm going home and reading the gospel of John tonight."

I looked at my watch. "You might wait until morning."

"No, I'm so excited," she replied. "I have to do this tonight."

I don't know how the Lord continued to work in this woman's life, but I have no doubt He was calling her to Him that night. I view our exchange as a small miracle because effective witness always depends on the power of God. The more I gave my testimony, the more I realized that evangelism in the natural order of things is an impossible task and a tremendously humbling one. God must do the convicting and the saving. Only God knows what's in a person's heart and how best to call that person to Himself. The most we can do is be available as an instrument of God's purposes.

This requires willingness. After my own spiritual reawakening, I was certainly willing, and my willingness soon grew into a passion for evangelism. Passion drew me on toward something deeper and more threatening still — abandonment to God. This, I began to see, was the key to being the faithful servant Jesus speaks of who multiplies a hundredfold the talents with which he's been entrusted.

The prospect of abandoning myself ever more completely to God made me hesitate. I had to ask myself whether I truly wanted to entrust myself to the Holy Spirit to be used in ways that were surprising and at times frightening. They were frightening because I was giving up control of "my life" in ways that were increasingly unpredictable. I didn't quite know who I was becoming, but I was certainly crossing frontiers from which there might be no return, and part of me was unsure whether I wanted *everything* to change. I wondered whether my life as a lawyer and an entrepreneur would retain any meaning. Surely, there was some value in what I had already done, besides its role in bringing me to my knees before God.

□ □ □

Nancy and I began to help organize future evangelistic dinners. Many of these were smaller gatherings that we hosted in our home. We became close friends with the key couples behind these efforts. The spiritual wasteland of our community concerned all of us, and we began to pray about what could be done beyond the Executive Ministries gatherings.

In this way the "host couples" — as we dubbed ourselves — joined together as a circle of seven couples. We met regularly to pray and look for opportunities to evangelize and minister. We've been doing the same now for over twenty years. From the beginning, we were an ecumenical group. Three of the couples were Catholic, two were Presbyterian, one Episcopalian, and one Baptist. One of the original families moved to Pennsylvania and was replaced by a couple who attended an evangelical community church.

One of the first things the host couples did was bring a ministry called FOCUS to the area's high schools. This program provides mentoring and Bible teaching for high school students in a fun and exciting format. FOCUS started in England's private schools and then spread to the prep schools of the East Coast. It's similar to the American-based ministry Young Life. (FOCUS has left our community, but Young Life has taken over its role.)

Then one of the women in our prayer group, Arlyne Lane, helped bring Bible Study Fellowship to the Grosse Pointe area, and she became the teaching leader. Her group rapidly expanded from a handful to 250 and then began subdividing as it branched out to neighboring communities.

Another couple, the Bolls, was heavily involved in Christian Business Men's Committee. Together John Boll and I took over organizing the Grosse Pointe Prayer Breakfast that continues to this day and attracts hundreds of people each year.

Next we started a retreat for business and professional people, bringing them together for a weekend in the spirit of Jesus. This became a yearly event, and the host couples have continued to sponsor it for the last twenty-three years.

In the true evangelical spirit, I was constantly thinking of activities and gatherings that would attract like-minded groups and focus their attention on what it means to follow Jesus. I started facing the fact, somewhat reluctantly, that I had talents as a leader and organizer.

□ □ □

I never understood how many people notice others' behavior until I began behaving differently myself. Simply the fact that the Lord led me to give up drinking for a time had a huge impact all by itself. About two years after I stopped drinking, I was at a dinner with friends when the wine steward came around. Usually, I placed my hand over my glass. This time, the same still, small voice that said, "Why don't you learn to relax in Me?" suggested, "Why don't you have a glass?" So I did. (I've continued to drink alcohol moderately.)

The woman next to me virtually gasped, "You're drinking!"

"Yes," I said.

"But we thought you considered drinking a sin," she explained.

"You never heard me say that, did you?"

She said, "No, but you weren't drinking, so we thought you must feel that way."

I couldn't explain the specific function my not drinking had played for a time, but I realized how many people notice when you diverge from social conventions.

Another peculiar circumstance cued me to my new role as a leader. In the midst of a host-couple meeting, I noticed that people were deferring to my judgment. This surprised me because Nancy and I were younger than everyone else, and several of our friends had been serious Christians for much longer. "Why are you deferring to me?" I asked.

"Because you're the leader of the group," one of the women said.

"I'm not the leader. We're all equal."

"We may all be equal," the same woman said, "but you're the leader of the group."

I didn't set out to be the group's leader, but this exchange made me realize that I was a catalyst to others' actions. Of course, it helped that I had a staff that could get letters out and do nuts-and-bolts organization.

My leadership in evangelical efforts didn't mean that I did not receive direction from others, however. I was particularly influenced by the wisdom of Frances Carter, a member of our host-couples group. Like me, she was Catholic. She was, in fact, the first Catholic in my acquaintance who had a similar enthusiasm for God. Her desire to share her faith had been purified by long experience.

One day as we were talking, she told me something I badly needed to hear: It would be better — more godly — if I toned down my witnessing. I had to quit trying to force people into taking the heavenly chemotherapy. I shouldn't let my zeal to evangelize blind me to the person before me. "Think more of the individual," she said, "and less about 'the sale.'"

Her advice was corroborated in an unexpected way. Just before Christmas of 1984, Dick took me to meet Doug Coe, the person *Time* magazine recently dubbed—much to his consternation—the "stealth persuader." Doug leads an organization commonly referred to as The Fellowship, which he would say is not an organization but a family of followers of Christ. The Fellowship lends support as Congress sponsors the yearly National Prayer Breakfast. It also networks with people around the United States, and indeed around the world, many of whom are leaders, all in the cause of Christ. Some consider The Fellowship elitist because it works with leaders; but people in The Fellowship believe they are serving the poor by influencing leaders. When leaders become true followers of Jesus, they begin to act on behalf of the least, the last, and the lost.

As Dick and his wife, Donalda, Nancy, and I traveled to Washington, DC, to meet with Doug, I thought about how my life was changing. This was a whole different ride. Dick thought Doug might show me how the scope of what I was doing for Christ could be greatly enlarged. I was eager to help if I could.

Our party went to the Cedars, a nineteenth-century mansion built on the Potomac surrounded by seven parklike acres. An adjacent carriage house is fitted out with meeting rooms and offices. That day I met a parliamentarian from Indonesia, an exile from Cuba, and similar figures from around the globe who were there seeking to learn about Jesus. The place blew me away.

Dick and I had lunch with Doug and a prominent Washington lawyer named Jim Bell. There was also a former professional golfer, Jim Hiskey, who led a Bible study on the PGA tour. While we talked and ate, Doug's wife, Jan, took Nancy and Donalda off for a lunch of their own.

I was eager to find out what Doug would make of my own story and what advice he would give me. Dick thought my meeting Doug would have profound consequences—and he was right. As we ate, Dick told the others about me, complimenting my willingness to speak, describing me as an indefatigable organizer for the cause of Christ. Doug took all of this in without saying much.

In many ways—I think I can say this as his longtime friend now—Doug Coe is different. He has a particular anointing that allows him to connect with people, even when what he says makes no apparent sense to others. He's highly intuitive and has schooled himself so thoroughly in the teaching methodology of Jesus that he can be as abrupt and disconcerting as his Lord.

At the end of Dick's encomium, Doug looked at me and said, "Let me tell you something. A year from now, you probably won't even know Jesus."

What in the world does that mean? I wondered.

"They're going to use you up and burn you out," he went on. "You're wealthy, you're successful, you're Catholic. They're going to have you speaking from pillar to post, and you have no right to get up and speak."

My twinges about my newfound Christian status began resonating and then reverberating and quickly filled my mind with a nearly deafening confusion, as if two fists had just slammed down on a piano.

"My advice," Doug said, penetrating my mental din, "is to go home and learn how to love your wife. Learn how to love your children. Once you do that, the Holy Spirit will lead you."

That was it? That was what Doug Coe wanted me to hear?

The man who had been represented to me as one of the great leaders for Christ had spoken. I wouldn't know Jesus in a year? I would be totally disillusioned? What right had he to speak to me that way? I could not have been more disappointed.

I couldn't forget what he had said, though, and I went home and thought about it. On the Sunday morning following our meeting, I was outside the house, chopping wood on my newly laid brick driveway. I was pondering so intently what Doug had said that I missed the log I was aiming at and swung the axe straight into my new bricks. I dodged the flying cinders and told myself to concentrate. Then I did it again. Wham! Right into the bricks.

Was my aim in my Christian life as skewed?

Chapter Seven

Rediscovering Catholicism

After hearing Doug Coe's cautions, I began considering more deeply what my evangelical reawakening might have to do with my Catholicism. I took a step back from public leadership, declining most speaking invitations. I needed to improve my spiritual aim.

I sought help from the institution that had nurtured my faith since childhood, the Catholic Church. Within evangelical circles, I had experienced a genuine renewal, and I had delved deeply into the characteristic spirituality of evangelicalism as well. The way my new friends and I carried our Bibles everywhere, called each other "brother," made theological points citing specific and sometimes obscure Scriptural texts, and delighted in early breakfasts as occasions for prayer marked us as "super-evangelicals." Was this the only genuine spirituality to be found? Or were there Catholic traditions that might help me mature?

I knew without a doubt that what I had experienced among my evangelical friends was real and of God. Why hadn't I known more of this in the Catholic Church? Was it to be found there? Did I fail to hear the Church's true message because of my arrogance?

Many of my evangelical friends believed that Catholics might be Christians—but in spite of the Church not because of it.

Some of the men in my Bible study expected that eventually I would want to join a robust evangelical church, where I could be truly "fed" week by week in the Word. Eventually, when a group of evangelical and Catholic leaders known as Evangelicals and Catholics Together (ECT) issued a statement in 1995 declaring their common belief in Christ as Lord, my first spiritual mentor composed an open letter that disputed whether Catholics could be Christians and remain faithful to their Church's teachings.

That unhappy event was years away at the time. Still, similar attitudes were communicated by my evangelical friends in a myriad of subtle ways. When I met evangelical leaders such as Campus Crusade's Bill Bright, I could see that they were delighted with my conversion story, but their eyes dimmed when I spoke of being a Catholic.

I write of these difficult things in my own experience because there are literally millions of devout evangelicals and Catholics who find their separated brethren mysterious if not suspect. Many Catholics find the language of being "born again" and "saved" off-putting. They feel as if evangelicals are claiming a higher order of spiritual experience. Feeling excluded from the ranks of the born again, Catholics often adopt a condescending attitude toward evangelicals and become dismissive of "fundamentalists." Who are these Reformation upstarts to instruct members of the Church that has stood against the gates of hell for the last two thousand years?

On the other hand, many evangelicals believe that Catholicism is little more than Pharisaism—a religion of works—with a Christian veneer, backed by a totalitarian insistence on obedience to a morally corrupt hierarchy. They believe that Catholics are told they must earn their way to heaven and are kept in a perpetual state of anxiety about their eternal destiny. They think such grace-denying fears are perpetuated in order to ensure that the laity looks to the hierarchy as mediators of God's forgiveness. Many evangelicals ask, Don't they know that all Christians have *direct* access to the Father, Son, and Holy Spirit? Don't they know people cannot earn salvation but that it is the free gift of God? If grace be not grace, all is lost.

These views on both sides are ill-informed, which I'll address in due course. For now I want to point out how such assumptions deepen the pain inherent in the church's division. Since I began this project, I have hardly talked to a single person whose own story or the story of someone close does not bear on these issues. One woman was a cradle Catholic and now worships happily in an evangelical church. The fervor and zeal of the congregation contrasts to the going-through-the-motions liturgies of her upbringing. Still, she retains a lively memory of a kind teacher in a Catholic school who taught her to worship "in spirit and in truth." I could see in her eyes that she longs for a way to unite what she knew as a child with her present experience.

Others have recounted how branches of their families remain alienated over these issues. Converts from one communion to another can sometimes even be disowned by their families.

In my own case, I could not forget my childhood devotion to Jesus — the joy I had known as a Catholic Christian in a family that loved God. However much I had thought I had loved God before, I had never understood His depth of love for me and how much He wanted intimacy with me. He wanted me to realize that He was not only my God but also my best friend and that, through His love, all my love of wife, children, family, and friends would unite in Him and give me a godly relationship with them. The rocks and debris that had choked the spring of Christ's living water had been cleared. I could feel it flowing into every channel of my life and carrying me forward. I thought there must be a way to integrate the gifts of evangelicalism with those of Catholicism.

So I went to my parish pastor to talk over these matters. I told him what had happened to me, using evangelical terms. I had committed my life to Christ, been born again, and now wanted to grow into full maturity as a Christian. I was concerned at the lack of spiritual vitality in our community. Drug abuse and promiscuity were rampant among our young people. Many parents were hardly better, with lives caught up in drinking and materialism. I told the priest that a key thing for me had been studying the Scriptures—reading the Bible cover to cover and understanding its overarching themes as well as coming to know how the old covenant prepared for the new covenant of Christ. I had been reading the Vatican II documents and quoted from St. Jerome: "Ignorance of Scripture is ignorance of Christ." I was also concerned that as Catholics we did not concentrate enough on Jesus' redeeming work.

Finally, I asked for some advice. What should I do to mature as a believer? How could I help with the challenges the community faced?

In retrospect I can see how I came across as both confused and confrontational. At the same time, a fervent desire for a greater experience of God should not be taken by any Catholic priest as alien. But sadly, the priest responded, at least in part, as if it were. He was wary, I'm guessing, about what changes I might want to see in the parish and defensive about his role. I was so intent on what I needed to know in order to integrate my spiritual awakening with my Catholicism that I thought little about "politics" and diplomacy.

The priest warned me against becoming overly enthusiastic.

The Church certainly did not need another fanatic. I should concentrate on the humdrum but difficult business of being a good Catholic. If I wanted to do something extra, I might start by reading the daily lectionary. These readings consist of short passages from the Epistles, the Psalms, and the Gospels.

I acknowledged that as the basis for preaching and an aid to meditation, the lectionary was incomparable. But someone who wanted to be on fire for God had to study the Bible as a continuous document.

We did not part on the best of terms.

I met with similar reactions from Catholic laypeople. The following incident happened a bit later, but it illustrates the quizzical view most of my Catholic friends took of my newfound zeal. I had been a member of Detroit's Cardinal Club since my late twenties. The Cardinal Club devotes itself to praying for vocations to the Catholic priesthood and raising support for seminarians. One time, during the discussion period after a speaker's talk at one of the monthly dinner meetings, I started talking about all the wonderful things I was seeing the Lord do around the world: the conversions, the physical and emotional healings, the charitable works that made the love of God real to believers and nonbelievers alike.

A friend of mine, a truly good man, commented, "Mike, you really shouldn't talk about Jesus that way in public."

If not at the Cardinal Club, an organization devoted to promoting the work of Jesus through encouraging vocations to the priesthood, where would I talk about Jesus? Understand that Catholics like my friend were brought up in a religious culture where priests did all the preaching and testifying. In many Catholic gatherings, when someone asks a theological question, all eyes turn to "Father," the priest. Deference is always due to the clergy, but Catholics often expect that it's the *exclusive* prerogative of the priest to answer the question. Because many Catholics remain untutored in their faith and may harbor a lot of heterodox ideas, deferring all questions to priests can seem a good thing. In the end, however, it's a great evil. The laity has a responsibility to know the faith and to "be ready to give an explanation to anyone who asks you for a reason for your hope" (1 Peter 3:15).

The Catholic Church makes that as easy as possible by providing the new and authoritative *Catechism of the Catholic Church*. As the saying goes, "You can look it up." The *Catechism* is thoroughly biblical, extensively citing Scripture as the basis for every teaching. Believers in other communions may quarrel at points with the *Catechism*, but any fair-minded Protestant should be impressed by its biblical reasoning. Many who take the time to read it are shocked.

Two other events capped my dismay at the response of my fellow Catholics to my renewal. Nancy and I began organizing more and more evangelistic dinners, and we began inviting more and more Catholics from our immediate community. This must have resulted in questions being asked of our parish priest. People probably wondered what he thought of our approach, and he did not react favorably. He wrote a letter to the parish in which he branded me as a "fundamentalist" and warned his parishioners against my influence.

Nevertheless, some did find what I had to say helpful. I was invited to speak to the Cardinal Club—the same group where my friend and I crossed swords over speaking too personally about Jesus. I was the only member ever to receive such an invitation. This caused a division too, though. Many of the clergy who usually attended the Cardinal Club thought it inappropriate that a "born-againer" be invited to speak—even a Catholic "born-againer."

I had accepted the club's invitation, so I went ahead and prepared to give my testimony. A friend of mine was kind enough to offer to drive me from my suburban office downtown. I said he needn't bother, but he insisted. He knew this would be a difficult day for me, and he was right.

Another friend, the president of a creamery and a part of the Cardinal Club's inner circle, promised that he would be in attendance as well. "Mike," he said, "I just want you to know that no matter what anyone says, I'm going to be there."

As I stood to give my talk and walked to the lectern, I could see that the creamery president was missing. I didn't mind the empty chairs that the clergy usually occupied, but I was disappointed that this man, who had made a commitment, had not shown up. He probably had an emergency of some kind, I told myself; he was an utterly reliable guy.

Then just as I began speaking, he burst through the door and scrambled to the front, picked up a chair, and sat right before me. That was incredibly comforting and much appreciated. And the talk seemed to go well.

Immediately afterward, a lawyer who also serves the Church as a deacon, stood and said, "I'm ashamed that people would be afraid to come and hear Mike speak." Two of those in attendance that day joined a Wednesday-night Bible study I had started. One has gone on to heaven, and the other is still a loyal member.

In the midst of these ecclesiastical controversies, I was left groping for a way to understand the relationship of the evangelical tradition to the Catholic Church. I could not deny that my faith had been nurtured by both. I had an intense desire to cling to Catholicism, but my Catholic brethren's querulous reaction to my renewed faith wasn't reassuring.

I talked these things over with a friend of mine from high

school who had become a Jesuit. I told him about what I had experienced as a result of asking Jesus into my life as Savior and Lord.

"You're the second guy I've talked to who's had this experience," he said. "I don't know what it's all about personally, but there's this group called F.I.R.E., a Catholic group, that might help you."

"What does F.I.R.E. stand for?" I asked.

"Faith, Intercession, Repentance, Evangelism." Here was a Catholic group that believed in evangelism. I had to find out more.

One of the leaders of the group, Ralph Martin, had written a book called *Hungry for God*. The autobiographical sections of Ralph's book showed that his experience corresponded in important ways with my own. He had been brought up in a good Catholic family, as had I. "As a child," Martin writes, "I had a deep and personal relationship with the Lord. I loved him, wanted to be close to him, knew he loved me, and never wanted to offend him. I took him and Christianity seriously."[6]

Martin went through a time of doubting and rebelling during his college years. Through the influence of a faithful Christian friend at Notre Dame, he came to acknowledge his flight from the truth: "I had made myself the creator of my own universe, the lord of my own and others' lives, the arbiter of my own morality."[7]

He attended a Cursillo weekend, a program of spiritual renewal that began in Spain in the Catholic Church. The word *cursillo* means a "little course," and these courses consist of powerful weekends of spiritual teaching and worship. The Cursillo movement has spread from the Catholic Church to other denominations and has become a tremendous ecumenical force for spiritual renewal. On his Cursillo retreat, Martin reached out to Christ as I had at the Executive Ministries dinner. He asked God to "take over his life," to become his personal Savior. He saw his childhood faith and his spiritual rebirth as related: "It was not that I wasn't a Christian before that. I was for many years. But it [a life of total commitment] was beginning again."[8]

That made sense because I had experienced much the same. My childhood faith and my spiritual awakening seemed part of the same, if discontinuous, journey.

Hungry for God's discussion of prayer as the key to "going on with God," the fount of a continuing personal relationship, made me want to learn as much as I possibly could from Martin and those associated with F.I.R.E. They seemed to have a keen understanding that the power for living the Christian life comes from being born again or "born from above"—the latter being a closer translation of the Scripture. "Genuine Christian prayer," Martin writes, "begins with the realization of being reborn into the family of God, being sons of the Father, brothers of Jesus, indwelt by God's own Spirit."[9]

I heard that F.I.R.E was leading an evangelistic crusade, with talks to be rebroadcast via closed-circuit television at a college in Ft. Lauderdale. Nancy and I were at our winter home in Sanibel, Florida, at the time. I asked if she wanted to rent a plane and hop over to Ft. Lauderdale for a day's worth of talks. She was eager to join me.

Although Nancy had remained formally an Episcopalian as long as her parents were alive, she had graciously consented to rooting our family's church life in our local Catholic parish. We went to church each Sunday as a family. One year after her mother died, Nancy was received into full communion with the Catholic Church. Although she never found the division between

Catholics and evangelicals as worrying as I, she hoped to discover the gifts evangelicalism had brought us within Catholic circles as well.

That day, listening to the F.I.R.E. speakers, proved a turning point. In addition to Martin telling his story and drawing out its theological implications, Father Michael Scanlan, the president of the University of Steubenville (now Franciscan University of Steubenville), gave an amazing talk on the importance of repentance.

Father Scanlan had been trained at Harvard Law School before deciding to become a Franciscan. In his autobiography, *Let the Fire Fall*, he recounts how God led him to leave a life among government and business elites. He is utterly candid about how God called him from vanity and pride to a love that he found difficult to accept.

Scanlan has obvious intellectual and administrative gifts, which resulted in his being appointed dean of the University of Steubenville straight out of seminary and then rector of St. Francis Seminary. But the gist of his story did not reside in his accomplishments but in God's calling. His story was one of yielding himself more and more fully to Christ. Like Martin, Father Michael Scanlan made a breakthrough during a Cursillo weekend: "I began to know Jesus as my brother. I saw that I was *joined* to him intimately, even more intimately than to a flesh and blood brother."[10]

Scanlan talked about the importance of being grounded *in Christ*. "I experienced new power," he recounts,

> in some familiar passages in the New Testament. "For you have died, and your life is hid with Christ in God," says Paul in Colossians. That meant *me*, Mike Scanlan. *My* life, my life in the Spirit, is in my brother Christ Jesus.

That little phrase "in Christ" that appears so often in the New Testament took on new meaning. "I became your father *in Christ Jesus* through the gospel," Paul writes to the Corinthians. That's just not a poetic way of speaking, I realized. Paul really means that. "Have this mind among yourselves, which is yours *in Christ Jesus*," Paul writes to the Philippians. This suggested to me that many great gifts, including a mind other than the worldly mind we all possess, are ours simply by virtue of being "in Christ."[11]

As a result of this experience, Scanlan began relating to Jesus in a more intensely personal way. The secret to life, he found more and more, was not in finding what one wanted to do. It was in finding what God wanted and joining in His work. One could rely on the power of God, not one's own abilities, to accomplish this work.

At the time of the F.I.R.E. crusade, Scanlan and his coworkers at the university had just come through the most difficult years of that institution's renewal. At God's direction they had changed an embarrassingly secularized and demoralized Catholic institution of higher education into a spiritual powerhouse. Franciscan University continues today to be a beacon to all those who seek a renewal of true spirituality within the Catholic Church and in other denominations as well.

Sister Ann Shields gave the final talk of that one-day retreat. She had been a nun in a religious order that suffered, as so many religious orders did, from a profound spiritual confusion after Vatican II. Furthermore, it had been her personal erroneous conviction that God had started her off in her religious life and then it was up to her to go on by sheer dint of will. "I was practicing the 'enormous virtue' of self-reliance, the American ideal," she says, "but not the gospel ideal, which is, 'I count everything as loss, and in weakness, everything reaches perfection. I came to you in fear and trembling that you might know the glory that comes from God.'"[12]

Shields reached a crisis in her vocation where she doubted God's very existence. One day she was in her convent staring out the window at a cold, blue-shadowed February day. She asked God to make His reality known to her. "I turned from the window," she recalled, "and it was as if I had bumped into somebody's chest. I stepped back and went forward again and the same thing happened. I heard this voice, not audible, but in my head, and it said, 'Don't you know I've been with you all the time?' It was an inspiration, because I wouldn't have thought it on my own."[13]

At the retreat, Shields emphasized the importance of making Jesus Christ one's personal Savior. Even if one had been a practicing Christian for years, she taught, it remained a good thing—a gift—to reach out to God as one's personal Lord and Savior.

The more I read and learned from Martin, Scanlan, and Shields, the more excited I became as I identified with what they were saying. I realized that they had been raised up just like saints throughout the ages to evangelize, telling people of the absolute truth to be found in Jesus Christ. Since that time, I've met a legion of priests and laypeople who are quietly lifting up Christ in all areas of the Catholic Church, meeting Pope John Paul II's challenge to evangelize.

All of F.I.R.E.'s leaders had experienced times of crisis when they reached out to God and came to know Him more deeply as Lord. Like me, they had what my evangelical friends would describe as "conversion experiences." The leaders of F.I.R.E. would describe these as conversion experiences as well, although more in the sense of what Protestants talk about when they speak of "rededication."

The leaders of F.I.R.E, I came to realize later, were all associated with the charismatic renewal movement within the Catholic Church. Besides accepting Christ as personal Lord and Savior, they spoke of being baptized in the Holy Spirit or the release of the Holy Spirit in their lives as another key experience. This confused me, as I had no previous experience with the charismatic renewal within the Catholic Church nor with its Protestant and Pentecostal counterparts.

Clearly, though, the role of the Holy Spirit is key in the Christian life, as any Christian would acknowledge. This drove me to reinvestigate the teaching of the Catholic Church on how the Holy Spirit, as well as the Father and the Son, come to dwell within the human person.

After hearing the F.I.R.E. talks, I realized that the way the Scriptures had come to life for me and my zeal in evangelism were evidences of the Holy Spirit's renewed work in my life. I was by no means as far along in my spiritual journey as the leaders of F.I.R.E., but I knew what they were talking about, and I was overjoyed that I could now understand my own renewal within the context of Catholic theology.

Moreover, this was not just a matter of theology: It was an experience—a life—that others were living with me in the unity of the body of Christ. The leaders of F.I.R.E.—like those in the entire Catholic renewal—recognized the importance of true ecumenism. They accepted the spiritual emphasis of evangelicalism as a gift. They understood, as Scanlan put it, quoting from the Vatican II documents, that the Church *subsists* in the Catholic communion. The Roman Catholic Church by no means makes up the church in its entirety. Our Orthodox and Protestant brothers and sisters often follow Jesus more fervently than we do.

As I indicated previously, from the time of my first encounter with F.I.R.E., I made up my mind to devote a portion of my time and resources to specifically Catholic causes. I also began to pray earnestly for the Catholic Church in the Detroit area. If even a fraction of the Catholic laity in our city could experience a renewal of their Christian lives through the Holy Spirit, we could do so much to alleviate the suffering of the poor and the despair of the rich.

□ □ □

Ironically, my "spiritual director" during the following months, a role normally associated with Catholicism, turned out to be Doug Coe. He did not simply send me home to stew about his admonition to mature in the faith before accepting leadership positions. He kept in contact, at first by letter and then by phone. At one point he said, "Would you like me to disciple you?"

I said, "Yes, I really would."

He suggested that we compare our travel schedules so that when it was convenient we could arrange short stops in each other's cities. Every few weeks we'd meet at the airport, either National in Washington, DC, or Metro in Detroit.

Even before we started meeting in person, Doug wrote about St. Paul's theme of being "in Christ." Like Scanlan, Doug saw this as the key to the life of faith. He stressed the imitation of Christ as the hallmark of true spirituality.

He wanted us to study the Gospels together carefully, noting every action of Jesus and how He responded to different circumstances. He asked me to immerse myself in Jesus' public ministry, Passion, and Resurrection, as a means of allowing God to reform my character. The greatest witness, the most faithful witness, Doug taught me, came not from talking *about* Jesus. It came from *being* Jesus to the world.

As I began to follow Jesus seriously once more, I had little more than words. Doug's first instructions to go home and mature in the faith prodded me toward finding more of the reality behind the words. I needed to become much more like Jesus in order to represent Him faithfully.

In our study together, Doug and I concentrated on the incidents in Jesus' life. We looked at how Jesus, when tempted by the Devil in the desert, relied not on His own strength but on the character of the Father. He quoted Scriptures, particularly from Deuteronomy, that declared God's objective character. In this way, I learned that when temptations come I need to rely on a power far beyond my own.

We looked at the famous incident when Jesus was at a Pharisee's house for dinner. A sinful woman, likely a prostitute, came in and washed Jesus' feet with her hair. Jesus knew that the Pharisee had not extended Him the usual courtesies, and He also knew that letting the prostitute touch Him had disqualified Him as a prophet in the Pharisee's eyes. He knew that the dinner invitation had been meant as a trap—a way for the Pharisee to provoke some discourtesy from Jesus and so disprove Jesus' claims to authority. Yet Jesus waited until the Pharisee's condescension betrayed his false attitudes. Then Jesus spoke the unvarnished and disarming truth:

Do you see this woman? When I entered your house, you did not give me water for my feet, but she has bathed them with her tears and wiped them with her hair. You did not give me a kiss, but she has not ceased kissing my feet since the time I entered. You did not anoint my head with oil, but she anointed my feet with ointment. So I tell you, her many sins have been forgiven; hence, she has shown great love. But the one to whom little is forgiven, loves little. (Luke 7:44-47)

As Jesus forgave the woman's sins, He left the Pharisee to reflect on how his arrogance and condescension was preventing him from receiving the fullness of God's forgiveness and love.

In this and so many other incidents, Jesus drew people out, letting them reveal their deepest commitments; then He fearlessly spoke the truth when the moment was right. In my dealings with people, I needed to be more patient, not hitting people over the head with my spiritual hammer but letting them show me who they were, both the good and the bad. Then, guided by the Spirit, I might speak God's Word to their hearts.

In my studies with Doug, I also saw how frequently Jesus retreated to pray. He spoke of prayer as being more vital than meat and drink: "I have food to eat of which you do not know" (John 4:32). This spurred me to become ever more committed to drawing whatever authority God wanted me to wield from His direction and from the power of God Himself.

Then I saw the great compassion Jesus possessed, even for those who were intent on His destruction—and their own. As He prepared to go into Jerusalem to face death, Jesus looked out over the city from a mountaintop. He prophesied the city's fall, knowing that by AD 70 the city would be ground into dust by the Romans. He lamented, "Jerusalem, Jerusalem, you who kill the prophets and stone those sent to you, how many times I yearned to gather your children together, as a hen gathers her young under her wings, but you were unwilling!" (Matthew 23:37).

I wondered whether I could love even those who rejected me, those who meant me harm. That was the love Jesus was calling me to embrace. I realized I could not possibly love in this way.

I would have to rely on the love of God working through me in order to be a true follower of Jesus.

□ □ □

I needed every lesson Doug could teach me. When troubles provoked my deepest fears and anxieties, I tended to forget about being a "new creature" in Christ. What St. Paul calls the "old man" reemerged all too quickly.

My greatest worries during this time concerned my son. Despite counseling, and the positive changes he saw in his parents' marriage and in his father personally, Michael was more rebellious than ever.

In 1984, the summer before he left for college, he went with a group of kids on a chaperoned trip of the West. The group of recent high school graduates was closely supervised by wonderful, experienced people. The trip encouraged young people to treat their peers with respect and dignity—to step into early adulthood and its greater degrees of independence responsibly. The rules were so strict as to forbid boyfriend-girlfriend attachments.

Out in Big Sky country, drugs were found in suitcases owned by Michael and a friend. The two were sent to the airport and flown home immediately.

I was at a loss as to how to deal with Michael. He would be going off to college in the fall, and I hoped, perhaps naively, that he would simply grow out of the problem. Nancy and I were happy with his choice of school, Marquette University in nearby Milwaukee. It came as a shock that after all Michael's protests over attending U of D High he wanted to attend a Jesuit college.

His first choice had not been Marquette. He would have liked to have gone to Boston College, but there was no way I was sending him to school that far away. At that distance, we'd hardly be able to see him, and I could only imagine the trouble he might get into.

When Michael was looking at colleges, I asked a Jesuit friend of mine for a recommendation. He cited Marquette as a "good, conservative school." The whole family visited the campus briefly and liked what we saw.

We should have spent longer investigating, though, as I soon realized. When we visited Michael during the fall of his freshman year, we saw beer being served to undergraduates in the college cafeteria. I hadn't realized that the legal drinking age in Wisconsin was eighteen or that the sudsy culture of Milwaukee flooded the campus traditions. Although there were many fine things about Marquette, if a student wanted to make his college years there a party, he could have a roaring one.

Michael's grades that first year reflected his commitment to having a good time and little else. At the end of the spring semester, I read him the riot act. He and I settled into a summer-long battle, with Nancy shuttling between us as a negotiator.

I was worried about the effect Michael's behavior might have on Laura. She was growing up so fast, and I was worried about the older boys whose attention she had begun to attract. As she prepared to enter high school, though, she had a fantastic attitude. In fact, that summer at a camp on Martha's Vineyard she accepted Christ as her Lord and Savior.

I will always remember watching her play tennis that summer. How Laura's honey-colored hair and long, tanned limbs shone in the sun! I couldn't stand the thought of anyone violating such innocence. I didn't want her hanging around with her older brother or thinking that his troubled life was cool.

I became so worried about this that I talked seriously with

Nancy about kicking Michael out of the house and telling him he was on his own. He didn't listen to a thing we said anymore. He might as well find out what it was like to make his own way. I kept talking in this direction, building up a head of steam, becoming ever more intent on banishing him.

My attitude only made Michael more obstreperous. He was far more deeply into drugs than Nancy and I ever knew. He truly didn't see any point in life beyond having a good time, and the affluence of the culture suggested that the party need not end, whether he remained part of his parents' household or not. This was nearly reasonable. Plenty of kids in affluent American suburbs roam from house to house, "crashing" with their friends, living a vagabond life amid what looks like stability.

Nancy thought that the key to reaching Michael was in showing him unconditional love. She talked over the situation with Dick. At the next Bible study meeting, Dick said, "Today, I want to talk about a principle in Scripture: What profit a man if he gains the whole world and loses his own son?"

Needless to say, I sat there and suffered. That Dick managed to put his point across cleverly, spending the whole hour on the topic without ever alluding directly to our situation, only made the suffering worse (though I ended up grateful for his insights). By the end of the hour, I realized that there was no way I would ever walk away from my son. I would do whatever it took, die to my pride, suffer whatever blows came to me, in order that Michael be saved. That Bible study was a huge turning point for me. I saw that following Jesus truly meant the way of the Cross. It meant participating in God's redemption of the world through suffering the Devil's worst. Satan was indeed a roaming lion seeking whom he might devour.

□ □ □

The evidence of God's grace and the deeper understanding of the spiritual life that God was giving me began influencing my behavior more and more. The greatest instance of this was with Michael.

Early in the fall of 1985, Michael and I were standing in the courtyard at the side of the house. He was home on a weekend visit from Marquette. We began arguing, with the anger escalating more and more. Michael ended up screaming at me, which he capped by crying out, "I hate you, and I don't believe in anything you believe. I hate you and I will always hate you!"

I felt as if he had hit me in the face. I saw his anger at full force, the depth of his long-harbored resentment. Then God gave me a moment of extraordinary grace. Rather than losing my temper or fighting back, I said, "If you hate me, that's my fault, and I ask your forgiveness. I want you to know that I love you, and I will always love you as long as I live. I will never reject you."

As it happened, Nancy and I were giving a tennis party that night, and I just sat in the tennis house and watched the others. I couldn't participate; I felt immobilized. As soon as the evening ended, I went home and began to pray. I felt weighed down by my son's need for God. I prayed most of the night and I asked God for one thing. "Lord, I don't ever have to see it. But I have to know deep in my heart that You will save this boy," I prayed. "You are his true Father much more than I am. I realize You've only entrusted him to my care for a time—I'm only his steward in this life. I give him over into Your ultimate care, knowing that You alone know what's best for him. But as a father who loves his son, as You loved Your Son, all I ask is that You would save him."

Toward morning, I had a deep sense of peace. I told Nancy, "I really believe that God has answered my prayer. I don't ever expect to see it, but God has given me real peace about Michael's ultimate destiny, his salvation."

The next day, Nancy and I drove Michael to the airport for his flight back to Milwaukee and Marquette. Not a word was spoken on the way to the airport, and my heart felt like lead.

Michael got out of the car, kissed his mother good-bye, and walked through the doors into the terminal. Not so much as a nod in my direction. I was so heartbroken that I couldn't even drive away. I sat behind the steering wheel, trying to collect myself.

A moment later, Michael came back through the terminal doors, walking toward the car and over to my side. I thought he must have left something in the backseat. He knocked at my car window, and I rolled it down.

"Did you forget something?" I asked.

He didn't say a word. He just leaned in and kissed me. That was the beginning of the end of his enmity toward me. Though he was not thrilled about going to church with Nancy and me and honoring us in other small ways, he tolerated our requests. Our family togetherness wasn't great, but it was on its way to improving.

Chapter Eight

The Darkest Hour

When Michael returned for his sophomore year to Marquette in the fall of 1985, Nancy and I insisted he settle down and pay attention to his studies. At the same time, I committed myself to loving Michael and Laura unconditionally. This didn't mean acceding to their demands or countenancing bad behavior, but it did mean that I would accept the pain, as well as the joys, entailed in loving them. It meant that my life as a parent would be central to following Jesus, even if it meant the Cross as much as the Resurrection. I began to see more and more why Doug had advised me to go home and learn to love my family before preaching about Jesus to others. The family is a school in which we learn to love, and the lessons can be difficult, even agonizing.

All seemed right, though, or better that fall. Michael is incredibly smart and insightful about his natural abilities. He understood that he learned better than most by listening. He could pass his classes and even make better than average grades if he simply showed up to every class, which he started to do.

Now that Nancy and I were on the same page about Michael, we felt much less tense. For a brief time, Nancy had been the go-between in the battle that raged between Michael and me, and I should never have let her assume such a role.

Laura continued to be my joy. As a sophomore in high school, she stood five feet eleven with long hair that swayed in counterpoint to her willowy frame. Thoughtful and sweet, she also had plenty of spunk and didn't hesitate to stand up to me. She was a Timmis in her love of a good argument. Any trouble she got into came more from high spirits and exuberance than anything else.

That summer she had taken out her mother's Lincoln Continental on the private dirt road that runs in front of our summer house in northern Michigan. The road makes a loop in front of the community tennis court. It's a perfect place for someone with a learner's permit to practice . . . if the rookie driver takes it easy. Laura overshot a bend in the road and sent the car crashing through the sumac bushes into a field by the tennis court. I held her in my arms, and both of us thanked God that no one was hurt.

I wasn't the only one taken by Laura's natural beauty. She modeled young-adult fashions for a Grosse Pointe magazine called *Heritage*. A protective father like most dads, I kept a watchful eye on the boys—some of them years older than Laura—who tried to win her affections.

Laura accepted the change in her parents' faith far more easily than Michael. She participated in the FOCUS program during her freshman year, and she continued to grow spiritually. I was overjoyed that Laura's relationship with God was well established.

□ □ □

Although my commitment to Jesus was solidly intact, there were certainly struggles and challenges to maintain my faithfulness. At times I had inklings of the warfare in the heavens that St. Paul admonishes us to keep in mind: "For our struggle is not with flesh and blood but with the principalities, with the powers, with the world rulers of this present darkness, with the evil spirits in the heavens" (Ephesians 6:12).

That October I had a strange experience. I woke up in the middle of the night and sensed a coldness in the house and what seemed to me a spiritual oppression. Those who have had such an experience know that the feeling is almost palpable. The feeling dissipated, but I never forgot it.

A few weeks later, on November 6, 1985, I came home to find that Nancy was upset with Laura. She had overheard Laura talking on the phone with a friend about how she'd skipped school and lied to her high school counselor and gotten away with it. The thing that most troubled Nancy was that Laura seemed so pleased with herself. Laura had skipped school to sit in a car with a bunch of boys and smoke.

I feared a repeat of Michael's rebellion in Laura's life. I told her that this kind of behavior must stop immediately. I would accompany her to school the next day and meet with the counselor, where Laura would apologize.

This was not a happy episode but hardly the worst. The point Nancy and I wanted to make was simply that Laura's behavior had to change before it led to real trouble.

Nancy and I will never know and cannot fathom what went on in Laura's mind that night. All we know is that she was extremely upset by the prospect of having to face the school authorities and to endure whatever punishment ensued. She called her brother at Marquette that night quite late. He told her that she was just going to have to take the consequences. She'd be grounded, life would be awful for a while, but then the time would pass and life would go on. This was good advice. Michael certainly knew how to weather a storm. He didn't think Laura sounded particularly panicked, but it was late when she called, and he detected something in his sister's voice that troubled him. He imagines now that she wanted him to come home, to be her protector, although she didn't say that and might not even have known consciously that was her wish.

We believe Laura stayed up all night, became increasingly distressed and irrational, and decided upon a dramatic gesture that she never expected would have real consequences. Fatigue probably overcame her before she realized what must happen next.

The next morning when I got up at six o'clock, I heard Nancy's car running in the garage. I found Laura in the locked car with the garage door shut and the garage thick with fumes. I threw open the door and took a shovel and broke through the window. I let out a wail that echoed up and down the street.

Nancy came running, her face ashen, and we laid Laura on the driveway and called 911. She looked ghastly; her face was gray. Nancy thought she might already be gone. There was no note in the car or anywhere else; we could only think that Laura never expected to pass out.

The EMTs came and rushed Laura to the hospital. I believe they revived her in the ambulance. When we reached the hospital, we heard the prognosis wasn't good. After about an hour, the doctors came out and told us she was dead.

I collapsed, shattered by grief.

Yet the first words that came to my mind were these: "No trial has come to you but what is human. God is faithful and will not let you be tried beyond your strength; but with the trial he will also provide a way out, so that you may be able to bear it" (1 Corinthians 10:13).

We drove the short distance back to our home. The word had gone up and down the street, and the house was already full of people. When I walked through the door, another Scripture passage came to me. I had never memorized these verses, yet they came to mind verbatim: "My sheep hear my voice, and I know them, and they follow me: And I give unto them eternal life; and they shall never perish, neither shall any man pluck them out of my hand. My Father, which gave them to me, is greater than all; and no man is able to pluck them out of my Father's hand. I and my Father are one" (John 10:27-30, KJV). I knew my precious daughter was in God's hands. That knowledge would carry me through the first agony of mourning.

That day we had a plane pick up Michael from Milwaukee. When he arrived home, I embraced my son, collapsing into his arms, and both of us felt the strength of a tie that no estrangement could finally unloose.

In Grosse Pointe, our friends constantly surrounded us. I came to know and depend on what it means for fellow believers to be the body of Christ. They were Christ's love to us during this time. I cannot think how we would have survived without them.

A priest who had come to the house pulled me aside. "Mr. Timmis, I have to talk with you. What's going on here?"

"What do you mean, 'what's going on'?"

"It's not what I expected."

"It's not?"

"The atmosphere is so calm."

"That's because we are followers of Jesus," I said. "The peace you sense is His presence with us."

One of our friends appeared at our door and asked if he could simply come in and pray. "I'll leave you alone," he said. "Just let me sit in the corner and pray." He sat there for twelve hours, came back the next day, and sat and prayed again for another twelve hours.

We had a private funeral and then the memorial Mass on Saturday at St. Paul's. All through the experience, I had a strong feeling of the presence of Jesus.

Doug called and offered words of comfort. Only ten days before, he had lost a son to cancer. He said, "Mike, there's no way I can help you, but I can tell you this. When the pain becomes unbearable, just keep saying His name — Jesus, Jesus, Jesus — over and over again. That's the only way you can handle the pain."

I did pray Jesus' name over and over. I came to realize just how powerful the name of Jesus is. The greatest prayer may simply consist in calling on His name. This would eventually direct me into a whole different way of thinking and acting.

It was almost two years to the day between my spiritual reawakening and Laura's death. There had been too much of *me* in my relationship with Jesus and service for Him. For the most part, it had not been *Jesus in me* but *me and my Jesus*. Up until that time, I had remained in control. But now, for the first time in my life, I was truly helpless. Abandonment in God went from a challenge to my daily reality to being the only way I could continue living. It was either Him or nothing. He was in control and He loved me, and I had to trust in Him day by day.

I can remember somebody asking, "How could God do this to you?"

"God didn't cause this," I replied. "God is with us."

Evil must be blamed on the Evil One, and yet we are so ready to indict God for the Devil's work. I knew the Lord was, as the psalm says, an "ever-present help in trouble" (46:1, NIV).

I don't mean to suggest that our faith tranquilized the pain. Nancy and I were in utter agony. There were many, many times when we simply didn't want to live anymore. The first of these occurred after we flew Michael back to college in our private plane. Coming home we experienced engine trouble. We had an experienced pilot, and we knew he would do whatever could be done. But to us, our lives didn't seem to matter. If the plane went down and we perished, we'd be reunited with Laura that much sooner, which was our only wish right then. But God asked us to remain in this life, and the plane landed safely.

The following Thursday when I went to Bible study, a man whom I'd known for some time was there. He approached me and said, "Mike, I haven't cried in twenty-five years. I cried at your daughter's funeral, but I didn't cry for you. I cried for *me*. When I saw you standing firm in your belief in Jesus, I had hope for the first time." He knelt down right before me and said, "Lead me to Jesus."

Not only would we experience God's consolation, but we would also be involved in His redemption in a new way. God would use our experience of having lost a child over and over to bring people to Himself. When I say in my testimony now that only Jesus can replace the love of a lost child, I speak directly to the hearts of people with whom I share this tragic experience.

Besides our friends' many acts of kindness, we received one particular mercy through a friend's faith and her spiritual gift. Frances Carter, whom I've mentioned previously, prayed to the Lord for a sign that she could share with us as a comfort. She had a vision in which she saw Laura being held in Jesus' arms in our driveway. This might have been only pious, wishful thinking, except for one detail that troubled Fran: Laura had short hair in the dream. Laura had always worn her hair long, at least to her shoulders and sometimes to the middle of her back. Fran had no way of knowing this, but Laura's hair had been cut the day before she died. The detail that troubled Fran verified her dream as a comforting sign from the Lord.

The first six months after our daughter's passing were difficult but only a preview of the grieving to come. People react differently to such a profound shock. Often a person only recognizes in retrospect the many shifts in his or her behavior that stem from grief. Nancy has always loved books, but for more than a year she found herself unable to read for any length of time. I continued to experience more of the numbness that came over me immediately after the tragedy. I felt removed from people and places and had a sense of merely going through the motions.

Early the next summer, our family took a month-long trip to the Orient. We visited Japan, Thailand, and China. I thought it would be good to create new memories as a family and to be together for an extended time. It was absolutely the right thing to do and a good time under the circumstances. Michael wanted to draw closer; his anger had cooled. We were all able to talk, and even to pray, together. The exotic locales "erased our blackboards," so to speak, clearing away habitual thoughts and worries. We lived day to day, escaping from our painful world back home.

After our trip, however, depression rolled over me like a tidal wave. This admission may surprise some who know us. That's because I never showed my grief in public. Many had difficulty understanding this and wondered why I didn't grieve more openly. That simply wasn't my way.

Nancy and I talked very little about Laura's death together. Neither wanted to make it any worse for the other. We stayed united by virtue of our common faith. This would have been completely unimaginable earlier in our marriage. We also let each other find the sources of mercy that suited each other best. Nancy found a grief counselor, who helped her talk through her grief. He accepted her beliefs and was fascinated by the ability of her faith to sustain her, when many people in similar circumstances turned to pills and alcohol.

I plunged even more deeply into God's Word. I've always had difficulty sleeping, and my depression brought with it unrelenting insomnia. Hopelessness and dread caused me to keep many sleepless vigils. I begged God to let me die, to go and be with Him and Laura. If I could have only one more moment to be with her . . . the chance to say good-bye. Then I'd realize how selfish such a prayer was. Laura was with God. She knew the reality of being in God's presence. I'd turn then to the Scriptures and read until I found a passage that lifted the darkness and eased my spirit. It was as if God would put His hand on my forehead. In the margin by the passage, I'd write "L.T.," Laura's initials. Then I could get some rest.

A few months after Laura's death, I received a call from Jeannie Graham Ford, sister of Billy Graham and wife of evangelist Leighton Ford. Leighton and Jeannie had lost a son, Sandy, to cancer years earlier.

"Michael," she said, "I know how you feel. I know you want to die. Throughout Scripture, men and women of God have wanted to die after tragedy struck." Then she recalled for me the story of Elijah under the broom tree. Elijah's life had been threatened by Jezebel, and he ran into the desert to hide. "This is enough, O Lord!" Elijah said. "Take my life, for I am no better than my fathers" (1 Kings 19:4). The Lord first comforted Elijah with a ministering angel, who roused him from sleep twice to provide bread and a jar of fresh water. When Elijah was sufficiently rested, the Lord directed him back to Horeb, the mountain of God. He found a cave there where he once again fell asleep.

The Lord then came to Elijah and asked,

"Why are you here, Elijah?"

He answered, "I have been most zealous for the Lord,

the God of hosts, but the Israelites have forsaken your covenant, torn down your altars, and put your prophets to the sword. I alone am left, and they seek to take my life."

Then the LORD said, "Go outside and stand on the mountain before the LORD; the LORD will be passing by." (verses 9-11)

Then God revealed Himself to Elijah as a gentle whisper.

Jeannie pointed out that the Lord allowed Elijah to rest. He gave His prophet time to recover from discouragement and fear. But then there came a time when He roused him to get up and be faithful to his calling. Because Elijah was willing to do so, God revealed Himself to Elijah in a singular way.

"This is your time to rest, Michael," Jeannie told me. "But there will come a time when the Lord wants you to get up and serve Him once more. Only you will know when that is. But it will come."

After that call, I felt I had taken one step out of my own desert. Gradually, with God's help, I walked out of that arid landscape and once again began climbing the mountain of the Lord. God called me back to service, in ways far beyond my own imaginings.

My grief over Laura's death has never gone away, and I've reached a point where I don't want it to. Laura somehow is closer to me because of the grief. After twenty-two years, her loss is easier to bear now but never easy. Nancy and I look forward to the Resurrection, when we will once again be together with Laura. We are already with her in anticipation though not yet in time. Until that day, Christ holds her in His arms and we in our prayers and memories.

Chapter Nine

Healing and Hope

When I felt sufficiently healed to be involved in Christ-centered activities, such as helping the poor and teaching Bible studies, I was a changed man, not only because of Laura's death but also because of what I had been on my way to learning before she died. People sometimes hear something of my story, and the stunning event of our family tragedy, and conclude that my life as a follower of Jesus is a psychological compensation. Or to put it more charitably, they believe God gave me a mission through my daughter's death. But the mission came before the tragedy, and the way I see it, the Devil meant Laura's death to thwart the mission. The Lord, however, used it to teach me the meaning of the Cross. There was mercy in the experience, if a dark mercy. When my time under Elijah's figurative broom tree ended, I returned to the same spiritual path I had been on, with a greater sense of the way's difficulties and with a greater sense of compassion than I ever had before.

As Doug and I continued to study together, we again concentrated on the Gospels and the life and ministry of Jesus. We looked at His character traits and how to incorporate these into our own lives. To study Jesus, paradoxically, is to be directed to the Father, as St. John wrote, "When you lift up the Son of Man, then you will realize that I AM, and that I do nothing on my own, but I say only what the Father taught me" (John 8:28).

Jesus encapsulates the Father's teaching in the Great Commandment: "You shall love the Lord your God, with all your heart, with all your being, with all your strength, and with all your mind, and your neighbor as yourself" (Luke 10:27).

What's surprising about the Great Commandment is that very few Christians pay any attention to it. It's not an original saying of Jesus but a piece of conventional religious wisdom that both Jesus and those who speak with Him cited as common ground.

Yet the Great Commandment is the law of love that Jesus fulfilled perfectly on our behalf, both in His public ministry and as He laid down His life as a ransom for many. It's the perfection that Jesus calls us to in the Sermon on the Mount, when He commands: "So be perfect, just as your heavenly Father is perfect" (Matthew 5:48).

St. Paul makes this magnificent statement in Philippians:

> More than that, I even consider everything as a loss because of the supreme good of knowing Christ Jesus my Lord. For his sake I have accepted the loss of all things and I consider them so much rubbish, that I may gain Christ and be found in him, not having any righteousness of my own based on the law but that which comes through faith in Christ, the righteousness from God, depending on faith to know him and the power of his resurrection and the sharing of his sufferings by being conformed to his death, if somehow I may attain the resurrection from the dead. (3:8-11)

I took this as my prayer, to be conformed more and more into the image of Christ, and thus, by the power of the Holy Spirit, I sought to keep the Great Commandment in imitation of Christ.

This radically simplified my life. First of all, it turned evangelism from something that I did for—or to—other people into a transformation that I prayed God would accomplish in me. I needed to be continually evangelized and turned more and more toward God through the good news of Christ, in order to love God with my whole heart, mind, soul, and strength, and to love my neighbor as myself. Doug taught me—and this is a first principle of The Fellowship—that the only person we can really evangelize is ourselves, and only then by the grace of God through the power of the Holy Spirit. But if we see conversion—or if you like, sanctification—as a continuous process, begun certainly at a definite point but then unfolding throughout our lives, then we will be using our will in accord with its true purpose.

When we try to will other people into the kingdom, on the other hand, we can become manipulative and actually attempt to displace God for our own prideful purposes. I'm afraid early in my life as an evangelical Catholic, I had the mistaken notion that somehow it was up to me to convert people. God alone calls people to Himself: "And when I am lifted up from the earth, I will draw everyone to myself" (John 12:32). Through Doug's teaching, I came to see that all I had to do was lift up Jesus and He would draw people to Himself. I had to do God's work in God's way, not my own. I should concentrate on growing in the knowledge and love of Jesus and loving others in my words and actions, leaving conversion to the One to whom such a supernatural action rightly and uniquely belongs.

In many ways, this was a tremendous relief. I didn't need to have an agenda for anybody but myself. I could concentrate on cooperating with God's grace as I learned to love Him and others more and more.

□ □ □

In the winter of 1985, I attended the National Prayer Breakfast for the first time. The Fellowship enables the House and the Senate to put this event on. Members of The Fellowship also enable and support a House prayer group and a Senate prayer group.

I knew that President Reagan would be at the Prayer Breakfast, and I was excited about that, but I never expected the panoply of world leaders in attendance. I went with the Canadian group, and as a result I attended the international luncheon. Many ambassadors to the United States, other government officials, executives of nongovernmental organizations, and prominent foreign citizens were there. They were from countries that were predominantly Buddhist, Hindu, and Muslim, and yet they were all talking about Jesus. I was amazed.

At the Prayer Breakfast I had a simple and yet profound experience that seems, in retrospect, a prophetic sign of my life's future direction. I was to meet Dick in the area of the Hilton Hotel where afternoon tea is served. I saw a stylishly dressed European woman, an African man in a dashiki and ornately embroidered robe, and an Asian man in a business suit, sitting around a little table with their hands clasped and their heads bowed, praying together. It was so beautiful. And the words, "For God so loved the world that He gave his only begotten Son" hit me full force for the first time. God loved the *world*. Unconsciously, I had made God in my image—a white Irishman. I realized that God's love extends to people of every race and nation. I had to understand the image of God more accurately, viewing Him as the Creator and Father of people all over the globe. I was aware in that moment that this realization would play its part in my destiny, although I wasn't sure quite how.

My mind took a quantum leap as to what I should be doing. Nancy and I had been talking about how God had given us resources for a reason. We were in a position to do many things with God's blessings. The three people from different continents holding hands and praying together inspired me to think about global outreach. I realized then that I was truly a different man. There was no going back to the life I had once led. As to what God had in store, I had no idea, but I knew God was leading me into the greatest adventure of my life.

□ □ □

After the first Prayer Breakfast, Nancy and I started attending other Fellowship functions. In the fall of 1986, about a year after Laura's death, we went to a retreat for international participants at C-Lazy-U Ranch in Granby, Colorado, just across the Continental Divide. There were people from all over the world—Fiji, Peru, Bolivia, Ecuador, and African countries such as Tanzania and Ghana. Many were government or military officials or business-people trying to use their resources on behalf of the poor.

One day, as we were sitting at lunch, Doug motioned toward a man with us and said, "Mike, I want you to meet this Peruvian brother, Jimmy Crosby. Jimmy, tell Mike what you're involved with."

Jimmy Crosby and an outstanding group of friends from Peru were putting together a foundation that would one day operate a financial institution like the Grameen Bank in Bangladesh. The Grameen Bank was founded by Muhammad Yunus, who earned a doctorate in economics from Vanderbilt University. He invented the concept of a "microcredit" bank that extends extremely small loans to the poor, without requiring collateral, so that they can start their own businesses. Since its inception in 1974 as a response to the famine that ravaged Bangladesh, the Grameen Bank has loaned approximately 4.9 billion dollars in amounts that average about one hundred dollars.

Jimmy said to me, "Doug has told me about your heart for the poor and your eagerness to help them. Why don't you come and work with us? We're setting up a foundation, but we need money. Why don't you come and be part of us?"

Nancy and I considered this and took a trip to Peru to learn more. We found a society in chaos. Peru's government was in a death struggle with Communist guerrillas known as the *Sendero Luminoso*, or Shining Path. This group was Maoist in its ideology and absolutely without mercy, employing terrorist tactics, blowing up buses, shopping centers, schools. They had the infamous habit of executing their opponents in front of their families. While claiming to represent the poor, they waged war against any activity that might actually benefit the poor, because the faster Peruvian society devolved into chaos, the faster they might come to power.

In turn, the governments of President Alan Garcia Perez (1985 to 1990) and President Alberto Fujimori (1990 to 2000) employed repressive tactics that resulted in many human-rights violations. Trying to do charitable work in Peru at the time was like wheeling a vegetable cart through a firefight.

On our fact-finding missions, Nancy and I had bodyguards and were driven in unmarked cars with blacked-out windows. We couldn't get out of the car because if guerrillas became aware of our involvement with the projects we were sponsoring and saw us at the sites, they'd kill the workers at those sites. The Peruvian foundation helped build a school, and during construction the workers slept in the building so that it wouldn't be burned down.

The Shining Path fomented anarchy in the countryside by marching into towns, executing the mayor and other local officials, and ordering those who lived there to vacate within the week. They would then go back at the stipulated time and blow the village up, forcing people to relocate to Lima and other big cities. As a result, the number of shantytowns in cities skyrocketed and the human needs became overwhelming. Jimmy's Peruvian foundation did a tremendous amount of good and served as a vital Christian witness to those who had been displaced by the ongoing guerrilla war. Nancy and I were happy to contribute to the effort.[14]

□ □ □

In the winter of 1988, Doug asked me to go on a mission for The Fellowship. "Mike, I would like you to do something in faith," he said. "I want you to go to Poland."

"What am I going to do there?" I asked.

"I have no idea," he replied, "but you'll be picked up by some members of the Sejm, which is their parliament. They'll set up meetings, and you can see how you might be able to help the country."

"Doug," I said, "I'm a businessman. What can I possibly do?"

"I have no clue," he answered, "but I ask you to go as a matter of trust."

That evening, I told Nancy about Doug's request. She asked the obvious question: "What can you do there?"

I had no clue either, and yet I felt called.

Doug sent his assistant, Rick Malouf, a businessman, to travel with me. We were met at the airport in Warsaw by a member of the Communist-controlled parliament, Kasimir Morawski, who arranged my agenda. Morawski was part of the limited political opposition that the Communists allowed.

The first meeting did nothing to quell my doubts about the efficacy of whatever mission I was on. Morawski had set up a dinner in a countryside dacha, which thirty people attended. On one side of me sat a priest who was part of Solidarity, and on the other side was the local Communist official. The room was divided right down the middle along these lines—Communists to my left, their political opposition to my right. They didn't have a word for each other. The silence was disturbing and the whole affair bizarre.

Finally, someone stood up and made a toast—in Polish—and everyone knocked down a jigger of vodka. I wasn't drinking then, so I put the glass to my lips and put it down again. Another person stood and made a toast. Then another. Both sides took turns exchanging toasts, and after each the whole company knocked down another shot. It didn't seem so much a dinner as a political drinking game. I put my glass up to my lips and put it back down over and over. Pretty soon the priest on my right and the commissar on my left were tipsy, and they reached across me, hugging each other. This made *One Flew Over the Cuckoo's Nest* look sane. Everybody was patting each other on the back and having a great time, and I felt I had just been beamed in from outer space. Eventually, Morawski invited me to say a few words, which he translated, but by that time I'm not sure anyone was listening.

That night I prayed, "God, why did You bring me here? I really believe You wanted me to come . . . but why?"

Every day of my five-day visit, I had a full schedule of meetings, where I told and retold my story, simply trying to lift up Jesus. I went to the Sejm and started meeting with people in the cabinet. I had read James Michener's *Poland* on the flight over, and upon my arrival I was shown a documentary on the destruction of the Warsaw ghetto in World War II that made use of footage shot by the SS. I understood the heroic and sacrificial role Poland had often played in European history and was still playing by virtue of Solidarity and the pope it had given to the world, John Paul II. So I often prefaced my remarks with comments about how much I admired the Poles for what they had suffered, citing specifics. The politicians couldn't believe I knew so much about Polish history—thanks to Michener. It's useful to be a quick study.

One day, we attended a lunch at the best restaurant in Warsaw. There were about twelve of us there, parliamentarians and bureaucrats. The restaurant had a huge, multipage menu. Since I enjoy chicken, I searched for a chicken entrée. I found one, and so I asked the waiter, "Do you have this today?"

He said, "So sorry, we're just out."

I told him I would keep looking.

Everybody else asked, "What's the special?" And they all ordered it.

When the waiter came back to me, I asked after another chicken dish.

"Oh, I'm sorry, sir, we're just out of that," he replied.

"Well, I'll have the special then." That was obviously the only thing they had available.

I nudged my traveling companion, Rick, to follow my lead. But he remained oblivious. "I'd prefer something else," he said and asked about another item on the menu.

"So sorry, sir . . ."

I kicked him under the table.

"On second thought," Rick said, "I think I will have the special."

A collective sigh went up.

The lunch meeting progressed, the special was served, and it proved better than either Rick or I had imagined. Right in the middle of the lunch, a man walked in and came up to our table. Every head turned to him, and all became dead quiet. The man exuded intimidation and threat. It turned out he was the head of the Polish KGB, the secret police.

There was an empty chair across from me, and he sat down in it. He said, "I don't know why I was asked to come here. I would like you to know that I hate Americans. I think you're a stupid people. I think you're stupid because you won the war and now you've let the Germans and Japanese beat you economically. I think you're totally stupid people."

I was in shock—and my Irish temper began to rise.

"I'm here for forty-five minutes," the KGB man continued. "When my driver arrives, I will leave immediately. So you'd better tell me what you want me to hear, because I'll be going as soon as possible."

He spoke perfect English. He had served in the Polish embassy in Washington.

I was pretty upset, and I said, "Let me tell you why I'm not here." I drew a big breath. "I'm a businessman, but I wouldn't invest a dime in this God-forsaken country that is so backward." I watched his reaction to this. "I'm not Polish, I'm Irish. And the only reason I'm here is because God sent me."

"Who sent you?" he asked.

"God sent me."

"That doesn't make any sense," he said.

"You're absolutely right," I replied. "It doesn't make any sense, but that's why I'm here." I don't know who was more astounded, the head of the KGB or me. I couldn't quite believe I had said what I did.

Around the table, nobody moved a fork. My antagonist and I might have been the only two people in the room.

"I don't understand what you just said." His tone was grousing but also puzzled.

"The only way I can explain it to you is by telling what's happened in my life, because otherwise it will never make any sense." So then I told him my testimony.

He listened to all of it, without interrupting. At the end, he remarked, "This is an incredible story." His manner changed totally. He was still the bloodhound, but now he was on the trail of something he found intriguing.

His driver came to get him, and he ordered the man away. We talked for an hour and a half—just he and I. Nobody else at the table said a word, not even among themselves.

That was when I understood the power of the name of Jesus. In the years since then, I've gone all over the world and stared into the eyes of many ruthless men like this one, dictators, warlords, government ministers, and bureaucrats, people without any light in their eyes. Not one of them has ever failed to respond to the name of Jesus—even when I've stumbled over my words because of exhaustion and felt utterly incapable of carrying on a decent conversation, much less presenting the gospel. While most lawyers would spurn any notion of being a "mouthpiece" for anyone, I'm happy to be that for Jesus.

□ □ □

I was hoping to visit St. Stanislaw Kostka Church in Warsaw, where Father Jerzy Popieluszko had been pastor when he was martyred in 1984 for his support of Solidarity. Three security police officers kidnapped him on October 19. He was beaten, tortured, and finally murdered, his body dumped into the Vistula Reservoir where it was recovered on October 30. As a result, his church became an ongoing center for Solidarity activities, rivaling the Gdansk shipyards.

I had been told that my driver would probably be a KGB agent and that I should be careful about what I asked him. Still, I expressed my wish to visit St. Stanislaw. I asked more than once. Every time, my driver said, "No, we won't have time. We can't go there."

One afternoon we were driving back to my hotel. We dropped off Morawski and others riding with us. I never quite knew where we were during my entire stay, and suddenly we pulled up in front of a church. "This is Father Jerzy's church," the driver said. He pointed, indicating I could go in.

It was a rainy late afternoon. There were people kneeling and praying in the rain everywhere on the church grounds.

I walked into the church. A woman immediately approached me and asked, "Are you an American? Would you sign this?"

"What is it?"

"A petition for Solidarity."

I was glad to sign it, of course. There were Solidarity signs everywhere in the church, and people packed the pews, though no Mass was being celebrated. The people were simply praying — praying for their freedom. I thought, *Their freedom will come. It can only be a matter of time with faith like this*. And indeed, three years after my visit, the Berlin Wall fell. The East Germans, the Poles, the Hungarians, the Czechs, the Slovaks, and the peoples of the Baltic republics were all free. Free at last.

When I got back into the car, my driver was smiling. He was so pleased with what he had done for me, as was I.

The day before I left the country, I met with the vice president. The morning I was to leave, I picked up Warsaw's major newspaper, and there on the front page, above the fold, was a picture of the vice president and me. My Polish friends translated the caption: "American businessman comes to talk to the vice president about Jesus."

I now knew what Doug was trying to teach me by sending me on this faith trip. All the way home, I had a palpable sense of God's presence, even when two policemen and their German shepherds boarded the plane in Prague to make sure everyone's papers were in order.

While reading on the plane, I found this passage: "When they were few in number, a handful, and strangers there, wandering from nation to nation, from one kingdom to another people, He let no one oppress them, and for their sake he rebuked kings" (1 Chronicles 16:19-21). In retrospect, I believe God called me to Poland at that time to experience God's power personally through my meetings with officials and collectively through the faith of the Polish people. Personal change can indeed lead to collective and cultural change. The forces of history often seem irresistible, and yet God's will is greater.

□ □ □

In the 114 nations that I've visited, I've never had an argument—not one—when I've spoken on behalf of Jesus. I always ask the same question: "What do you think is the number-one problem in the world?" The answers I receive are never clear.

I reply that I believe the number-one problem in the world is alienation. Then I ask, "What do you think the answer is for the alienation of nation against nation, tribe against tribe, one person against another?" Never once in any country has anyone ever given me an answer.

I say, "I believe there is an answer. The answer is Jesus."

Never once has anyone replied, "That's ridiculous." Sometimes people are quiet and simply listen, keeping their own counsel, but no one has ever said, "I think that's stupid." Or "I reject that." Or "That's religious nonsense."

Likewise, I've never had anyone ask me what my denomination is. No one has asked me about what I do or how I do it. Even people I've visited many times, leaders I've visited through the years, never get very personal; they simply want to talk about Jesus and what He's doing around the world.

□ □ □

When I arrived back at the Detroit airport from Poland, I expected an enthusiastic welcome home from Nancy. Our marriage had undergone a deep renewal, and we were both thrilled to see each other now after even short absences. The trip had been life-changing for me, and I had so much to tell her. Nancy was kind and affectionate, but I could tell by her expression that something was seriously wrong.

"Honey, what's happened?" I asked.

"Michael's going to Africa."

I looked at her dumbfounded. Against all odds, Michael had been accepted into several law schools, scoring high on the LSATs. So why would he be going to Africa, and for how long?

"He wants to go for a year to do humanitarian work," Nancy explained. "I should never have talked up the Peace Corps."

"He's joining the Peace Corps?" I asked.

"No, he's just going on his own."

"Where?"

"Mozambique."

My heart fell so abruptly that I couldn't catch a breath. Mozambique was in the midst of a civil war. The State Department had issued a warning against Americans traveling there, and many commentators were comparing the situation to the Killing Fields of Cambodia during the Pol Pot regime. Michael knew of the needs in Mozambique because we helped support a missionary there, but for him to go just then might well mean his death.

When I arrived home, I went straight to the prie-dieu in our bedroom and knelt down. I cried out to God, "Lord, I can't handle this. I'm so afraid. I will die if I lose another child. The burden is too great for me."

I prayed long into the night, unable to sleep despite my exhaustion from the trip. Gradually, a deep sense of peace came to me once more. Somehow Michael would be okay. God was working.

Doug and his wife, Jan, came to spend Easter with us at our house in Florida, as they had for the previous couple of years. Doug and Michael hit it off this time, talking about my son's new favorite pastime, stunt kites. There's quite a lot of kid left in Doug, and he wanted to know all about the kites and why Michael enjoyed them so much. He shared his own life with Michael as well. At the time, he was writing two to three thousand letters every month, keeping in touch with people around the world. He had all their names and addresses on five much-thumbed Rolodexes and a minimal amount of secretarial help to keep track of this voluminous correspondence.

"Why don't you computerize it?" Michael suggested. "You could put it all on a database, and that way you'd be able to track when responses came in and your replies."

Doug thought that sounded great, but he didn't have the time or the expertise, and no one in his organization did either. Besides, back then in 1988, personal computers were a relatively recent phenomena.

"I could do it," Michael said.

"Would you?" Doug asked. "Would you really?"

"Sure," Michael said. "Sometime when I have a break. Maybe after graduation."

Doug and I spoke of Michael's wish to go to Mozambique, of course, and Doug was as alarmed as I was. He arranged for Michael later that spring to have lunch with a new contact of his, a Ugandan named Gordon B. K. Wavamunno. Gordon was the lone Mercedes-Benz dealer in Uganda, where he did a thriving business selling cars to the government and embassies. Doug thought that by placing Michael with Gordon, he could direct my son out of harm's way and let God do something in their relationship. The country was then recovering from Idi Amin's and Milton Obote's reigns of terror, and Doug thought this presented an opportunity for witness and ministry.

As Gordon spoke to Michael of his home in Uganda, he described a huge house on Lake Victoria, a fishing boat, and horses quartered at a nearby farm. Michael thought he might well enjoy his humanitarian work a lot more if he could fit in some fishing and horseback riding in a country known as the Switzerland of Africa.

Summer came, and Michael graduated from Marquette. Doug was expecting him at the Cedars to work on the proposed database. Michael thought he had been indefinite enough in his responses not to be taken seriously. But Doug, Nancy, and I had taken him very seriously.

"I don't want to be cooped up with a bunch of holy rollers," Michael said, in protest.

This time Nancy put her foot down. "You gave your word."

"They don't really want me there," he said.

"If you are going to break your word, you make the call. You're the one who thinks your word is so important," Nancy said, knowing Michael hated hypocrites above all things. "Just call and say that you're breaking your word. You've promised them, but you're not going to come. Because I'm not going to do it for you and your dad's not going to do it for you. Just be a man and do that."

"Okay, I'll go," Michael said. "Just buy me an open ticket on return, because as soon as I'm done, I'm out of there."

Michael flew to the Washington, DC, area, and Nancy and I headed to our home in northern Michigan, where we prayed fervently for God to touch our son's heart at the Cedars.

□ □ □

Michael told us that when he arrived at the Cedars, he felt immensely uncomfortable. The people around him were talking nonstop about Jesus, while his thoughts ran to the hash pipe he had hidden away. Michael had allotted about four days to construct Doug's database, but as he started the project he found enough work to last four months. He didn't know whether he could last at the Cedars for more than a week.

Michael did make friends with a Pentecostal pastor from South Africa named Nick Maputo. Nick spoke to him not at all about religious matters, but about world music and the African scene.

The spiritual crisis that Michael felt closing in on him prompted one disturbing thought: What if Christianity turned out to be true? He had always considered himself a seeker after truth—although, sad to say, his Jesuit education was so influenced by higher criticism and other forms of skepticism that his truth-seeking impulse had nearly been stanched. Michael thought he would give God a try, though, and resolved to read the Bible and pray for a week and endeavor not to sin.

At the end of the week, Michael went with others in residence at the Cedars to a Pentecostal church in downtown Washington. He enjoyed the rocking gospel music. He felt like he was in *The Blues Brothers*. As the pastor preached, he whipped up the congregation into an emotional frenzy, and members of the congregation began jerking and jiving and literally doing some of that holy rolling Michael had so disdained. People shouted out in tongues. Women fell around him left and right, slain in the Spirit.

Michael's one thought was, *I gave this a week, and now I see I've let myself in for a charade. This isn't real.* He was furious.

As he stood in his pew, though, closing his eyes against the frenetic scene, the Lord spoke to him. He experienced what Catholics call an inner locution, plain and strong: "Your days of drugs and pain are over, My son."

The Lord then showed Himself to Michael, gave him a glimpse of what it means for Christ to be the Logos, the creative plan of the universe. Michael felt that God was showing him His plan, and a stream of images developed out of one another at the speed of light, as if the history of creation were being rerun. Michael knew God was real, more real than anything else he had ever experienced. Even having been given this vision, he knew he could reject what God had shown him — the option was his. But Michael felt that he himself had been recreated in Christ, as the Logos gave him a moment of insight into how all things came to be. He felt there was nothing to do but worship this God.

Michael went back to the Cedars and threw away his drug paraphernalia. He hasn't gotten high since. He's truly a new creation in Christ.

□ □ □

Shortly thereafter, Doug called me. "Are you sitting down?" he asked.

"Okay, I am now," I said.

"I've got news for you that you're not going to believe, and you may not be happy about it," he said. "Mike has asked the Lord into his life."

"Really?" I nearly shouted.

"Yeah, it's just amazing," Doug said. "A South African pastor befriended him. I don't know what else happened, but somehow the penny dropped. Michael has met Jesus. But he met the Lord in a context that's not your context—a Pentecostal church. He's pretty excited about the Pentecostal experience."

"As long as he's met Jesus, I don't care how he's worshipping." The words were tumbling out, I was so excited. "Just meeting Jesus is everything."

God had fulfilled His promise in a way I never expected. A kid from Grosse Pointe was befriended by a pastor from South Africa and met God in a downtown Washington Pentecostal church. Talk about the God of paradoxes! The same joy that I felt when Michael was born was the joy I felt when he was born again.

Chapter Ten

Ambassador of Reconciliation

Despite the amazing events that occurred during my 1988 trip to Poland, I had no inkling that expedition would open up a new dimension of life. It was the beginning of nearly twenty years of global travels as an ambassador of Jesus. In the next three years, from 1989 to 1992, I visited Bangladesh, Belize, Burundi, the Cayman Islands, Chad, Costa Rica, Cuba, Djibouti, the Dominican Republic, the former West Germany and East Germany, Grenada, Guatemala, Guinea Bissau, Honduras, India, Iraq, Laos, Kenya, Nepal, Nicaragua, Niger, Pakistan, Peru, Puerto Rico, Syria, Thailand, Tibet, Turkey, Uganda, Venezuela, Yemen, Zambia, and other nations.

My travels continue to this day. I have now visited well over a hundred countries, talking with everyone from world leaders to the poorest of the poor. I know more about what I'm doing in these countries than when I first went to Poland, but essentially I continue to perform the same mission as I did that day with the head of the KGB: I talk about what Jesus has done for me and how in Jesus we find the world's one true hope of reconciliation.

One of the first trips I made in conjunction with The Fellowship remains vivid in my memory. We prepared a year in advance, setting up a trip to twenty-one countries in twenty-one days that began in August of 1989. U.S. Senator Dave Durenberger, a Republican from Minnesota, and Congressman Tony Hall, a

Democrat from Ohio, accompanied Doug and me—and other companions, who joined us from time to time—on a trip to Europe, the Middle East, the Indian subcontinent, and several African nations.

We took turns explaining why we had come to believe that the world's greatest problem was alienation—among families, communities, and nations. The mission of Jesus was to reconcile us to God. To the extent that humanity could be reconciled to God through Jesus, the world's problems could be overcome. In every nation to which we traveled, from Syria to Thailand, from Niger to Nepal, we were always received with courtesy and complete freedom to express our beliefs.

As we traveled, Doug sometimes extended invitations to the National Prayer Breakfast to leaders who seemed open to learning about Jesus. When we found a core group who believed in healing divisions through prayer, we encouraged the formation of leadership prayer groups. Occasionally, the way would be open to prompt a prayer breakfast within an individual country or among a group of countries. If leaders would meet together and seek God's wisdom, solutions never before envisaged might appear. This is the greater part of the gentle diplomacy that The Fellowship encourages around the world.

The 1989 trip was chock-full of memorable experiences. I'll never forget meeting the Dalai Lama at his residence north of Dharamsala, India, where he has lived in exile since the Chinese occupied Tibet in 1959. The Dalai Lama is a charismatic figure—very warm and friendly, and he speaks excellent English. We were directed to call him His Holiness, which we did. We were also instructed never to touch him.

At the beginning of our meeting, we listened to the Dalai Lama talk about being the reincarnation of the Buddha of

Compassion—the "Kundun," or "The Presence." Eventually, we asked him who he thought Jesus was. He became tremendously animated and said that Jesus was the greatest teacher who had ever lived. We then had quite a discussion about what Jesus taught and the meaning of His being God's Son. At one point, the Dalai Lama told us that he had learned about who Jesus was and about the West from a monk named Thomas Merton. Did we know of Merton?

For many years Doug, two other friends, and I had spent Holy Week at Gethsemane Abbey outside Louisville, Kentucky, where Merton lived. I had been an avid reader of his work for years, particularly his spiritual autobiography, *The Seven Storey Mountain*.

I asked the Dalai Lama if he had read many of Merton's books. He said he hadn't read any, noting that Merton died on the way home from a visit with him, cutting short their friendship. I told the Dalai Lama that I happened to have a copy of *The Seven Storey Mountain* in my camera bag. Would he like it?

"I would love to have it," he said.

I apologized that it wasn't a new copy; in fact, I had annotated the margins, comparing my own thoughts to Merton's.

The Dalai Lama, whom I wasn't supposed to touch, cupped one hand on the back of my neck and said, "Your words will make it even more precious to me."

Later in our trip, we had another poignant meeting, this time with the leader of a Muslim nation. We often took turns speaking at these meetings, so that everybody had a chance to talk about their beliefs. This day I was asked to share the story of my journey to a personal relationship with Jesus as we were seated in the president's office. In the middle of my presentation, he broke down and began to weep. It was absolutely amazing how touched he was. In the years to come, we were able to meet with him again to study the Bible together, and an abiding friendship resulted.

Another time, we met with Mother Teresa, who had just turned seventy-nine. She was incredibly generous with her time. Her famously direct and simple manner came through immediately. I'll never forget her taking Tony Hall's right hand and touching each fingertip as she voiced each of these five words: "He did this for me." Then she did the same with his left hand as she said, "I do what for Him?"

"The poor are a gift," she told us. "We have received much more from them than we give to them."

At the same time, she insisted she was not a "social worker." "If I do just social work, it takes me away from Jesus," she said. "I am not a social worker because of Jesus."

Instead, she practiced identification with the poor as part of her total surrender to Jesus. "We must have total surrender — trust completely," she said. "How can I help the poor if I don't take a vow of poverty? God has to show His greatness through nothing."

Mother Teresa told us that she asked herself every night what she had done for Jesus that day. She insisted that the key to her life was the time she spent in prayer. Along with her other sisters, she prayed four hours a day, rising at 4:30 each morning to spend two hours in prayer. Another two hours were devoted to prayer later in the day. She tried to pray continually as well, while walking, cleaning, or caring for the poor.

She told us, "Christ said on the cross, 'I thirst.' What He was thirsting for was the love of the people. The aim of our order is to satiate the thirst of Christ on the cross. I will satiate the thirst of Jesus by working for the salvation and sanctification of the poorest of the poor."

She took us on a tour of her clinic and the order's orphanages.

She wanted us to see the lepers they were caring for, saying how beautiful she found them. She told us about a Muslim afflicted with AIDS who came and said, "I want to die like the people who have accepted Christ die." So he was baptized before death.

As we walked along the corridors of the clinic, she went up to person after person and touched them, offering comfort. As she moved from room to room, she was a shining light that radiated the overwhelming presence of Christ to everyone around her. I have never felt so humbled as I did in the presence of Mother Teresa, her assistant Sister Priscilla, and the other beautiful nuns of the Missionaries of Charity.

□ □ □

A few of my missions on behalf of The Fellowship have had specific aims. In 1991, I flew to see the president of Serbia, Slobodan Milosevic. This was at the beginning of the Balkan War, when the former Yugoslavia broke apart and the Orthodox Serbs and the Catholic Croats began the war that would soon engulf the Muslim Bosnians.

My friend Clark Durant and I met with Milosevic in Belgrade. Our purpose was to invite him to a private, unpublicized meeting at a house in Switzerland. A member of England's House of Lords, a member of the French parliament, and one from the American Senate, as well as a few friends from The Fellowship had already agreed to attend. We hoped President Milosevic, President Franjo Tudjman of Croatia, and President Milan Kucan of Slovenia would attend as well. We wanted to draw together the presidents of the warring Balkan republics so they might talk and pray together about peaceful solutions.

Before visiting Milosevic, Clark and I toured hospitals in

Belgrade, which were already filled with amputees and other wounded soldiers. We carried with us a letter from a U.S. senator whom Milosevic knew that stated we had a message from him to convey. The message was, of course, peace through reconciliation in Jesus.

We met with Milosevic in his office. A chain smoker, he blew smoke into the air, forming a thick cloud. He said sharply, "You have only fifteen minutes. So what do you want to tell me?"

I shared about Jesus for fifteen minutes. When he didn't stop me, I kept going, and soon forty-five minutes had passed.

At that point, Milosevic asked, "Why have I never heard about Jesus in this way? Do you know anything about me?" I said I did. I knew among other things that his father had been in an Orthodox seminary and had committed suicide.

By this time, Milosevic had warmed considerably. He kept inviting us to smoke a cigarette with him. He asked, "Would you share what you have just told me with a good friend of mine?" He popped out of his office and returned with his foreign minister, Vladislav Jovanovic.

The meeting lasted two and a half hours. Milosevic agreed to the future meeting of presidents and other officials—a secret peace summit, of sorts. He gave me his home telephone number so I could be certain of reaching him. As we left the meeting, we were elated. We thought of the wounded soldiers we had seen in the hospitals. Many might now be spared a similar fate.

After we came home, we made additional contacts. But we did not hear anything further from President Milosevic's office. Because the meeting was fast approaching, I made a determined effort to reach him. I called repeatedly during a thirty-six-hour period. Each time, I was told that the president would call me back. But the last time I phoned, I was told not to call anymore.

I have thought of this incident over and over again. The massacre of Srebenica, the sieges of Sarajevo and Kosovo, the genocidal "ethnic cleansing" of the Bosnians, and the displacement of massive Croat and Serbian populations—all of this might have been avoided. Some would say that I went on a fool's errand. After all, Slobodan Milosevic proved himself one of the twentieth century's most ruthless butchers. A few might think that I should never have even spoken to him. Members of The Fellowship have in the past been criticized for their willingness to talk with such leaders. Some believe such efforts provide "religious cover" to tyrants and are an encumbrance to government diplomacy. And some use guilt by association to discredit The Fellowship.

I am comforted by Mother Teresa's insistence that we are responsible for being faithful, not successful. I think of St. Paul's witness to various government officials in the book of Acts. On several occasions, they listened intently and were almost persuaded, yet finally they would not act against their political instincts. I also recall Jesus' telling silences at His trial and Pilate's washing of his hands.

What if Milosevic had come to the meeting? In the end, I'm glad to have facilitated such a historical possibility. I intend to go on doing the same, as I'm able.

□ □ □

Sometimes such efforts bear fruit. In 2001, friends of The Fellowship family helped bring together the warring leaders of Rwanda and the Congo, which led to a peace agreement. That's only one example among many of why President George H. W. Bush saluted Doug as an "ambassador of faith."

As followers of Jesus, we are called to be peacemakers.

Sometimes our efforts are successful, sometimes they are not. But we should always be faithful to our calling, doing whatever is necessary, regardless of the results.

Chapter Eleven

Called to Serve

Even as I began to travel the world, telling leaders about the love of Jesus, I became ever more concerned about the Catholic Church in my home community. Vatican II called the laity to proclaim the Word of God alongside the clergy and to join with Christ in a new way in His work of redemption. Church officials at the highest levels talked a great deal about the "new evangelization." Through F.I.R.E. and its leaders, particularly Ralph Martin and Father Michael Scanlan, I had discovered with joy the characteristic gifts of evangelicalism within Roman Catholicism. But neither the true role of the laity nor the intimate experience we can have with Jesus was being taught in many of our parishes.

I know that it's awfully difficult for the clergy to hear such statements and even more difficult to take remedial action. Many Catholic parishes, even fairly large churches, are staffed by one priest. He's charged by his bishop with ensuring that nothing is taught contrary to Catholic belief, particularly in regard to faith and morals. The Church has depended for so long on a "one-person-shop" style of governance that many clergy cannot understand the type of lay leadership that plays such an important role in Protestantism. Suggestions like this to priests can sound like a request to take on yet more responsibility. By the time they baptize, do funerals, officiate at weddings, and take care of the sick, there's little time left for anything else. For these and other reasons, Catholic clergy often have a visceral reaction against lay leadership, particularly when it comes to teaching fundamentals about Christianity.

Once, during the years when I was praying for Catholic renewal, particularly in Detroit, I was invited to speak at a prayer breakfast in Wichita on the theme "Following Christ in the Marketplace." This was an ecumenical event. Because I was a Catholic, the organizers invited the bishop of Wichita. I've been told by someone who knew this man well that he was an outstanding churchman who emphasized having a personal relationship with Jesus Christ. The bishop sat next to me on the dais.

He remarked to me, "You know, Mr. Timmis, it is very unusual for a Catholic to speak so openly about his faith."

"Yes, I understand that," I said. "I didn't used to do this, but then I realized I was failing the Church as well as myself."

He seemed to take this in stride.

Then I added, "But I have to say in all honesty, Bishop, that speaking about my faith was never taught as part of my obligation as a Catholic. Are you teaching this in the Diocese of Wichita?" I have reason to know now that he was, against much resistance. But he turned abruptly to the person sitting on his other side.

After my talk, this good bishop came up to me and said, "Mr. Timmis, I want to apologize to you. I didn't understand. Now I understand."

In many instances, Catholic teaching has been decimated by what's called the "social gospel," which teaches that Christianity consists of working for justice. It tends to minimize or neglect altogether the transcendent and supernatural basis of the faith. Supporters of this belief system emphasize Jesus as a cultural and political reformer, and they strongly encourage social activism as a means of bringing society ever closer to utopia.

Unlike the social gospel, the Great Commandment puts the love of God first: "Thou shalt love the Lord thy God with all thy heart, and with all thy soul, and with all thy strength, and with all thy mind" (Luke 10:27, KJV). Then comes the command, which is "like unto it" but not synonymous: "And thy neighbour as thyself." The love of God, who more than returns that love, must come first. Otherwise, when life comes down to a contest, as it often does, between your interests versus my interests, my self-interests are sure to win out. We cannot love our neighbors as ourselves — much less fulfill Jesus' command to love our enemies — without the love of God being in us.

Even where the social gospel has not displaced the true gospel, Catholics often receive the misleading impression that Christianity is all about being good. The Church's worship needs to be complemented with people *talking together about their faith* — that we will be saved by our faith in Jesus Christ who died for each of us on the Cross. Millions of Catholics in America go to Mass week after week, shake hands with the same people sitting around them at the passing of the peace, saying, "The Lord be with you," and shake hands with the priest at the end of Mass. These same millions never say a word to one another about why they believe what they believe. Their only contact remains confined to handshakes. They never discuss the Scriptures. They never relate problems they're having at work or in their families to their faith. They sometimes believe, as we've seen, that they shouldn't talk openly about their faith in Jesus, even in religious meetings.

In contrast, the Scriptures say, "For, if you confess with your mouth that Jesus is Lord and believe in your heart that God raised him from the dead, you will be saved" (Romans 10:9). As

Catholics, we believe fervently in the Resurrection, but we rarely confess that "Jesus is Lord," except during the recitation of the Creed. We rarely breathe a word of it otherwise, not to each other and not to our neighbors.

As a result, going to church for many Catholics is a cultural experience. We believe in God, we believe in Jesus Christ as our Savior. But we go to church, we worship, and then we leave and continue on with a life that's divorced from the experience we've just had. Too many Catholics exist in this state of unacknowledged indifference.

There's a tremendous need all over the world for Catholics to understand what it means to have a personal friendship with God—to understand their scriptural birthright. The only way that can come about is through renewal. Where there is renewal, there is recommitment and changed lives. For renewal to happen in full measure, we have to talk with one another about what we believe and how it relates to our lives.

□ □ □

God eventually gave me a role to play within the Detroit Catholic community. He did so despite my arrogance and critical spirit. In 1990, when Archbishop (now Cardinal) Maida replaced Cardinal Szoka in Detroit, I was invited to a welcoming party for him. The party took place aboard a sixty-foot yacht—a beautiful craft with sleek lines that sat high in the water. About a dozen men and the newly elected archbishop boarded the boat in Grosse Pointe and then cruised up Lake St. Clair to a private club for dinner. The other men congregated in the main cabin, while I hung back at the stern, sipping a drink and looking out over the beautiful waters that I love so much. I was in a strange, down mood. I felt out of it.

Archbishop Maida noticed me sitting by myself and spoke with me. "Why are you out here alone?" he asked.

"I just really don't feel like I belong here," I said.

"Why not?" he probed.

"I feel like a hypocrite."

"You do?" he said. "Are you a Catholic?"

"Yes."

"Do you go to church?"

"Yes," I replied. "In fact, I go to Mass every day."

"Every day, I see." He looked away for a moment, considering. "What do you think of the Catholic Church in Detroit, then?"

"Archbishop, you have to realize I'm the Catholic I am today because of the evangelical movement and its influence on the renewal. These things showed me what Catholicism really means."

"That's very interesting," he said. "I'd like you to come and talk with me."

"Okay, if you want me to." I thought perhaps he was just being courteous.

He became more emphatic. "Call me and we'll have lunch or breakfast together."

"Okay," I said.

My tone must not have been sufficiently earnest, because he grabbed my shirtfront and twisted his fist, drawing me close. "Listen, Mr. Timmis, I don't think I'm anything special. You come talk to me."

The rest of the night, I was in a mild state of shock. When I arrived home, as I began my night prayers, I felt the presence of God. I thought about the way I had behaved and was ashamed of my arrogance. I don't normally make promises to God, but that night I told the Lord, "Father, if You'll just give me one more chance, I'm going to say the rosary every day for a year and offer my prayers on behalf of the evangelization of the Archdiocese of Detroit." (As it happened, this promise resulted in a daily prayer practice that has continued for over sixteen years now.) I wanted not only to tell the archbishop what was on my mind in a candid and authentic way, but I also wanted the chance to do something for the cause of renewal.

The next day, someone from the archbishop's office called and asked if I could come down that next week and have breakfast with him. Unfortunately, I was going out of town, but we arranged a date for when I returned.

On the morning of the breakfast, I was driving downtown to the archbishop's residence, anticipating an inquisition. I imagined him surrounded protectively by five or six priests.

The archbishop's secretary, a young priest, met me at the door and told me the archbishop was waiting for me in the dining room. I found him alone at a nicely set table.

He greeted me warmly. "Sit down. Eat, please." There were rashers of bacon, a serving dish with scrambled eggs, covered baskets filled with muffins and sweet rolls, and a platter of fruit.

Despite the archbishop's cordiality, I remained anxious. "I don't want to waste time eating, Your Eminence. I just want to talk with you."

"Okay, start at the beginning," he said.

I told him my story, keeping it as brief as possible. He responded with what I would come to know as his characteristic magnanimity. "I accept what you say, Mike, and I feel much like you do. I'll make you certain promises, but then I want you to promise me a few things as well."

I was ready for him to fire away.

"You have to understand that I'm the archbishop of all the

people in Detroit," he began. "I'm not the archbishop only of the consecrated or of renewal Catholics or of any other particular camp. You see what I'm saying. I'm not even archbishop of Catholics alone. Evangelization, as you've pointed out, also involves creating a humane culture for people who don't share our beliefs. So I'll never be able to move as fast as you might like. That said, I'll do anything you ask me to do, but you have to promise me one thing: You will never embarrass me. Because if you embarrass me, you embarrass the Church, and I can't have that."

I nodded in agreement.

"I would also like your promise that you'll come help me," he continued. "I want to help the poor, and I know you have a heart for the poor. Come help me with the poor, Mike."

When Archbishop Maida's appointment to the Archdiocese of Detroit was first announced, he had made a speech before the Detroit Economic Club, which has hosted every president since Richard Nixon, as well as major presidential candidates, international leaders, and the heads of the world's largest corporations. The club also has often served as a forum for these community leaders to launch major initiatives. Archbishop Maida spoke to the club about the gospel imperative to "make all things new." He spoke of programs he wanted to come into being.

"I envision," he said, "a number of schools that are not Catholic but are Christian, truly Christian, Christ-centered." He wanted to establish ecumenical magnet schools in the most impoverished areas of Detroit that would serve not only Catholics, but any family that desired a Christ-centered education for their children.

At our breakfast together, he again mentioned his idea for the schools. "I'd like your help with this project," he said. "It hasn't really gotten started yet, but I want to include you in the first organizational meetings."

I told Archbishop Maida I'd be glad to help with these schools. As I've mentioned, Nancy and I served on the board of the Grosse Pointe Academy, which Michael and Laura attended for elementary and middle school. That had prepared us to be involved with such a project.

Also, when I became a partner at the law firm, I felt very strongly that we should begin sharing our blessings with others. To this end, we had decided to befriend an inner-city family. Through a priest friend of ours, we were able to contact a recent widow, an African American named Marie, with five children. When I called and asked if we could come visit her, Marie told me she wasn't interested in any relationship with a limousine liberal, but if we wanted to become her friends, she would like that.

We did become great friends, and through that friendship we were able to help Marie from time to time. For example, her mortgage was sold to another mortgage company, and they attempted to raise her interest rate, which was against the law. I was not only able to stop this abuse in her case, but I also referred the whole matter to the attorney general of Michigan. That stopped the practice generally.

So I felt Nancy and I knew something about school governance, and our friend Marie had taught us at least something about the challenges and needs of inner-city families. I was more than happy to tell Archbishop Maida that I'd be glad to help.

The Lord was answering my prayer, I felt. In the space of two pivotal meetings, I'd gone from being a Catholic who had been marginalized because of his zeal to someone called upon to pitch in and help.

□ □ □

Not long afterward, I received a call from the archbishop's office. In the process of familiarizing himself with the archdiocese's condition, Archbishop Maida had discovered some disturbing information. The local church wasn't taking care of its retired priests in a manner that allowed them to live with dignity. Many of them had opted out of Social Security—as was their right as clergy—in order for the Church to extend its resources as far as possible. Now they could barely put food on the table. In addition, the archdiocese's seminary and parochial school system were in great need. The diocesan inner-city schools were particularly hurting.

Archbishop Maida asked me to help with a major capital campaign. He had already recruited John J. Riccardo, the former chairman of Chrysler Corporation. The archdiocese also had contacted a group called Community Counseling Services (CCS). They had an excellent track record in designing financial campaigns for large nonprofit organizations, and they thought the archdiocese could raise sixty million dollars. They advised rolling in an ongoing funding effort called Catholic Service Appeal (CSA), which brought in about fifteen million annually. They considered the seventy-five million–dollar total an ambitious but viable goal.

Archbishop Maida was excited and a bit daunted at the prospect. As I sat in the meeting and heard the company's report, however, I had one thought: *No way.*

I asked if I could speak to the archbishop privately. He and I, along with Riccardo, adjourned to another room.

I said, "You shouldn't do this."

"What do you mean?" the archbishop asked.

"First of all," I said, "you already have the fifteen million from the Catholic Service Appeal campaign. You don't want to roll that into anything. You want to keep it separate. I know they are telling you that CSA will suffer if you don't, but I don't believe it."

"Okay," he said slowly.

"Secondly, you've got to go for one hundred million."

The archbishop blanched.

"Archbishop, you have to understand that people my age love the Church and relate to it differently from the next generation," I said. "I went to a Catholic grade school and high school. I understand the Church and its needs. My generation has never been asked to give anything—not in a substantial way. There's a huge amount of wealth, Catholic wealth, in this archdiocese. If you don't call on us now, that wealth may not be available in the future. We're dying off. You've got to ask now, and you've got to ask for the full amount needed."

"Do you really think one hundred million is possible?" he asked.

"Absolutely—through the grace of God," I answered.

Riccardo backed up what I was saying. Then we went back into the general meeting with the CCS people.

"There's been a little change in our thinking," the archbishop announced. "We're going to raise one hundred million dollars. And we're not going to roll in CSA."

I'm sure the professional fund-raising people were thinking, *There's no way.* They didn't want to announce a target goal that wouldn't be reached and then be blamed for an unsuccessful campaign.

During the course of the fund-raising, we did several smart things, including giving parishes an incentive for contributions by specifying that a certain percentage would be returned to each parish that met its goal.

The short version of the story is that under the outstanding leadership of Archbishop Maida, what was called "Stewards for Tomorrow" raised 104 million dollars and giving to Christian Service Action actually increased at the same time.

□ □ □

Soon Archbishop Maida wanted a steering committee to meet to forward his vision for ecumenical, Christ-centered magnet schools for inner-city Detroit. He asked my friend Clark Durant to chair the committee and church leaders from other denominations and businesspeople like me to participate.

I couldn't always attend the meetings because I was traveling internationally a great deal and still overseeing my law practice and business. When I called the archbishop to let him know of an impending absence, he said, "Why don't you send Nancy?" So she became involved, and we had a wonderful time working on the project together. She brought her own experiences on the school board to the project as well as her expertise as a former teacher.

The committee included blacks, whites, and Hispanics. We started meeting together with the idea of founding a cluster of primary schools and one middle school that would exemplify the best in Christian education. From the very beginning, we also wanted these schools to present business leaders with an opportunity to invest their time in mentoring children.

Our committee meetings did not go well on all fronts at first. Some members had trouble with the schools being called "Christ-centered." They preferred ambiguous language about encouraging good values. But Clark, Nancy and I, and others agreed that true ecumenism can be found only in Christ. I remember saying, "If it's not Christ-centered, then there's no use doing this. It's going to be nondenominational, but the teachers are going to be

Christ-centered, and we are going to teach the Bible every day."

After the winnowing of those who disagreed with a Christ-centered approach, about twelve of us remained. We became the first board. We then had to confront all the organizational difficulties. Father Bill Cunningham, who had started an enterprise called Focus Hope to help the poor acquire job skills, provided some much-needed direction. "Let me tell you something," he said. "If you wait until you have everything figured out, you will sit here and beat this thing to death. There's only one way to get this started—and that's ready, fire, and aim."

We still had to raise the money. The archdiocese gave us a school it could no longer run. The Lutherans gave us two schools. Our family joined with three other families to pledge the necessary funds to finance the schools for three years. (From that point to this time under Clark's dynamic leadership, we have raised well over twenty-five million dollars for the schools.) The schools in Detroit are named Cornerstone. Nancy and I suggested this name because that is the name of the schools that our family had established in Uganda.

There are now four Cornerstone grade schools and a middle-school campus in operation. Dan Rather at CBS, *The Wall Street Journal*, and many others have done stories about the project. Ninety percent of Cornerstone alumni graduate from high school, compared to approximately 34 percent in all the urban schools. Much of Cornerstone's success, I believe, is due to its "partners program"—families, individuals, and businesses giving scholarships to individual students and meeting periodically with their student at the school. Partners encourage their students to believe that they, too, can do great things in life.

□ □ □

In 1994, Archbishop Maida was elected to the College of Cardinals. Nancy and I were able to attend the Consistory in Rome, which was a great privilege. Our association with Cardinal Maida has grown into a tremendous friendship. I consider him one of the most deeply spiritual men I have ever known. From the very first, when he grabbed my shirt and told me he didn't consider himself anything special, he has consistently lived his commitment to servant leadership. He doesn't think of himself as a "prince of the Church," but as a shepherd who has a deep love for Jesus.

Cardinal Maida has spent many times with our family, and he's baptized all of our granddaughters. We talk frequently on the phone and his mother and brother, who is also a priest, have become friends of ours. I never presume on our friendship, but I value it as one of my life's great gifts.

□ □ □

As I was being accepted more and more within Catholic circles, I was asked to become a Knight of Malta. The Knights of Malta began as one of the military orders and were first known in the thirteenth and fourteen centuries as the Hospitallers of Jerusalem. They have evolved into a fraternal organization devoted to helping the poor in the Holy Land and around the globe. They sponsor ultrasound machines in crisis pregnancy centers, set up medical clinics in distressed areas, purchase medical supplies, and run soup kitchens.

At first, I wasn't sure whether to accept the honor. When I told Cardinal Maida about the invitation, he said, "Mike, you can't evangelize from without. Renewal has to come from within the Church. I think you should join. It would help establish your credentials as a Catholic leader and enable people to invite you to speak in places where they might not otherwise."

So Nancy and I became respectively a Dame and Knight of Malta, kneeling before Cardinal O'Connor in St. Patrick's Cathedral in New York.

□ □ □

One of the most exciting things in the Catholic Church is that there's a young and growing group of priests who are on fire for the Lord. The new vocations that I see are very powerful. For instance, for many years Nancy and I attended a Catholic parish other than our own, St. Lucy's. There, we were really fed by the great ministry of Father Bohdan Kosicki.

In the mid-1990s, a new pastor, Father Leonard Blair, was appointed to our local parish, St. Paul. Before we had even met, he called me. "I just read an article about you," he said.

"Really?" I asked.

"Yes. I want to congratulate you," he said. "I think it's wonderful that a Catholic is on the board of Promise Keepers. Why don't you stop in and see me?"

Blair had been secretary to Cardinal Szoka in the Vatican before assuming the pastorate at St. Paul. He asked me how I became involved in Promise Keepers, a mostly evangelical organization. (That's a story I'll tell in a later chapter.) "I think that's wonderful," he said, "and I want you to know that I support you and your friends."

Blair, who rather quickly became an auxiliary bishop, was a wonderful pastor as well as a true academic, with a dry sense of humor. He worked first on the physical restoration of St. Paul, adding a greeting space without destroying the essential integrity of the French Romanesque architecture.

Then he called to say, "You know, Mike, I feel very guilty. Here I'm saving the physical aspect of the church, but I'm not reaching out spiritually, in the sense of mission, to our parish. Would you help me pick some speakers to come and do a parish mission?" (A "parish mission" is like a revival—usually four days of nightly meetings devoted to conversion and renewal.)

"I would be honored to do that, Bishop," I said. So I asked the leaders of Renewal Ministries—Ralph Martin, Sister Ann Shields, and Peter Herbeck—to come preach the mission.

The church was still under reconstruction, so we met in the gym. Eight hundred people turned out every night. As always, the leaders of Renewal Ministries did a fantastic job, inspiring the people of St. Paul to claim the richness of their Catholic faith as God's love for them.

That night I felt that the story of my place within the local church had come full circle. The "fundamentalist" and his wife were now the people entrusted with choosing those who would provide instruction for our parish.

Opportunities for teaching and other ministries by the laity are increasing, and our parishes are coming alive. When I went through my own renewal, few of the parishes in the Detroit area had Bible studies. Now almost every church does. I can see what has happened in Detroit spreading throughout the country as a holy fire.

Chapter Twelve

The True Source
of Strength

Once I truly committed myself to being a follower of Jesus, I began to rediscover the wealth of guidance in the Catholic tradition. Besides the sacraments, there are two great aids to informing our minds and hearts about God's intentions for the world and our own place in His plans: reading the Scriptures and prayer. I know that the life I lead, with a dizzying variety of responsibilities, would simply be impossible without the power God bestows through the Scriptures and prayer.

The classic Catholic text *The Cloud of Unknowing* tells us that God's Word is like a mirror. Just as we cannot see a smudge on our faces without the help of a mirror, we cannot see the spots on our conscience without looking into the Bible.[15] Reading the Scriptures and prayer go together as we pray through the Scriptures and the Scriptures teach us to pray.

For the last fifteen years, I've been engaging in prayer disciplines that aim at the biblical injunction to "pray without ceasing." Taken literally, that sounds impossible, and even what I'll detail as my own practices may initially seem too demanding. I recommend beginning as the Lord leads—perhaps devoting as little as five minutes a day to prayer—and then follow where He leads.

I start each morning by confessing my sins. "Oh, my God, I am heartily sorry for having offended Thee." Then I say the Lord's Prayer, centering every day, as Jesus did, on the Father.

Next I call upon my "prayer team." I believe that the body of the church of Jesus Christ is undivided; that there's one church, consisting of those who are alive and those who are with the Lord. As we see in the book of Revelation, those who are presently with the Lord pray before God's throne. So I ask people who are close to me—Nancy, Michael Jr., Doug, Chuck Colson, and my accountability group, Clark Durant and Chuck McLeod, and many others—to pray with me. I also ask my daughter, Laura, my parents, and two women I witnessed to before their deaths to pray with me. I ask saints such as the Blessed Virgin Mary, Simeon and Anna, and others among that "great cloud of witnesses" we are surrounded by to pray with me. I don't pray *to* those who stand before God's throne any more than I pray to my present Christian friends. It's a matter of intercession—that they pray with me to Christ our Lord.

Depending on how early I've risen, I'll then read morning prayers out of the devotional magazine *Magnificat* or a similar publication, *Conversations with God*. These devotionals include the daily Mass readings from the Bible, liturgical prayers, and short devotional essays. I pray through the early morning as I dress, shower, have a cup of coffee, and get myself off to daily Mass.

If I have time, I'll at least begin the Rosary. For me, it's like putting on classical music that relaxes me and enables me to move into a deeper level of the mind and spirit, opening myself up to God. I've had most of the greatest revelations of the will of God in my life when I've been praying the Rosary.

As I'm praying the Rosary, I meditate on the mysteries of

God's action in the world. When I meditate on the Crucifixion, for example, I think about the love Jesus demonstrated for me in His ultimate sacrifice and the sacrifice of the Father in permitting it to happen. I realize that my sin caused Jesus' crucifixion, and if I were the only person in the world, He would have died for me. That's how much Jesus loves me.

I attend daily Mass because the Eucharist and the Word of God are central to my day, and without them I would not feel complete. As a Catholic, I believe that the Eucharist sustains the very life of the church. As the *Catechism* teaches, "The Eucharist is the efficacious sign and sublime cause of that communion in the divine life and that unity of the People of God by which the Church is *kept in being*. It is the culmination both of God's action sanctifying the world in Christ and of the worship men offer to Christ and through him to the Father in the Holy Spirit" (emphasis added).[16]

The Eucharist leads my heart toward the Lord's own as nothing else does. It's the summit of my prayer, because what else is prayer but coming into the presence of the Lord? And what is the end of all of our lives but doing the same and hearing the proclamation, "Well done, thou good and faithful servant"? All of life should be what can be experienced in eucharistic worship—a continual communion or being with God. "I have been crucified with Christ," St. Paul declared, "yet I live, no longer I, but Christ lives in me; insofar as I now live in the flesh, I live by faith in the Son of God who has loved me and given himself up for me" (Galatians 2:19-20).

The worship of the Lord in the Mass is a profoundly evangelical act as well, as the name of the rite comes from its commissioning role. It's called the Holy Mass because "the liturgy in which the mystery of salvation is accomplished concludes with the sending forth (mission) of the faithful, so that they may fulfill God's will in their daily lives."[17] Every time we celebrate the Eucharist, we are sent out to accomplish our part in God's mission.

□ □ □

As I go through my day, I call upon the Scriptures I've memorized and the traditional prayers I've known since I was a boy to keep centered in the Lord. Traditional prayers are a wonderful aid in this practice. For example, I love the "Anima Christi," attributed to Saint Ignatius of Loyola:

Soul of Christ, sanctify me
Body of Christ, save me
Blood of Christ, inebriate me
Water from Christ's side, wash me
Passion of Christ, strengthen me

I also spend time in thanksgiving. Sometimes I'll go through my own personal litany, the list of God's blessings to me, and just say "thank you." I try to do this on a regular basis so I'm not always standing before the Lord with my hands out.

It's so easy to drift away and get caught up in what displeases God without even knowing it. That's our tendency toward sin that St. Paul acknowledges when he laments that the good he wants to do he doesn't do, but the evil he'd like to avoid he goes right ahead and does anyway (see Romans 7:19). So I not only spend time examining my conscience, but I do so in a systematic way throughout the week. I try to train a searchlight on every hidden corner and shadow.

On Mondays, Wednesdays, and Fridays, I examine my conscience on the basis of the seven deadly sins: lust, spiritual laziness, anger, pride, envy, greed, and sins of self-indulgence. On Tuesdays and Thursdays, I appraise—as well as I'm able—the fruit of the Spirit in my life: love, joy, peace, patience, kindness, generosity, faith, meekness, and chastity. On Thursdays and Saturdays, I reflect on the gifts of the Holy Spirit: holiness, counsel, perseverance, wisdom, understanding, and knowledge. With all my failings, I still remind myself, "I am holy because He is holy and He is in me."

Once I finish my examination of conscience—and because these patterns are habitual they go quickly and are not as onerous as they might appear on first reading—I petition the Lord for various blessings. First, I pray for my family—every day. Then I pray for the Catholic Church, that God would unify it, purify it, and renew it. And I pray for all true believers, that we would be one, just as Jesus Himself prays in John 17. I pray that we will work together in the cause of Christ.

□ □ □

I frequently go to Confession—or the Sacrament of Reconciliation, as it's now called. Telling what I have discovered about myself to another human being makes me own up to whatever insights I've gained. It also leads many times to unexpected discoveries, because our ability to deceive ourselves—both in our virtues and in our failings—is endless.

People wonder about confession being humiliating. It can certainly stir feelings of embarrassment, but baring your soul to another human being is simply humbling in a salutary way. It allows for the realization of God's love and forgiveness as nothing else does.

My evangelical friends ask why I don't confide my confession to God alone; after all, it's He who forgives us. That's true. The priest doesn't forgive our sins; he pronounces God's pardon. But if I find it too daunting to confess my sins to another person, how much more so should I find confessing them to God? The priest, by acting in the person of Christ—as His surrogate, so to speak—helps me understand far more powerfully the reality of God's love.

Confession is a powerful means that God uses to make His presence known in my life. When we clean out all the sinful garbage, the soul becomes a fit habitation for the Lord, and the Holy Spirit can go to work. Unless the Holy Spirit is active in our lives, we have no power to live for God.

□ □ □

My prayer practice took about five years to evolve from advice I received and practices I discovered or recaptured on my own. It has been relatively stable for the past fifteen years. I used to have tremendous trouble with being distracted, though. I'd start to pray, and then my mind would start to race, thinking about the things I had to do or some small incident that had happened.

I once asked a good friend, a priest named Father Duane Stenzel, "When you're praying, do you get a lot of distractions so that it's really hard to keep focused on your prayer?"

"Yes, I do," he said.

"How do you overcome that?"

"I don't," he said. "Every time you force your way back into prayer, into focus, what you're really saying is 'Jesus, I love You.' Sometimes I say 'I love You' over and over when I'm praying, because of my distraction."

Now when I'm praying and meditating and I get distracted, I go back and repeat, "Jesus, I love You." That discipline has helped me to be much more focused than I used to be in prayer.

The graces that come with discipline in prayer and frequent use of the Sacrament of Penance are enhanced through one-on-one spiritual direction and the spiritual friendship to be found in small accountability groups. I've had three fine spiritual directors, or mentors, in Dick Robarts, Doug Coe, and later on, Chuck Colson. In the long term, I've found that an accountability group suits me best in adhering to the narrow way. Two friends, Clark Durant and Chuck McLeod, and I meet regularly to discuss our present challenges. For a time, the three of us had our offices in the same building, and we met at least once a day, if not more. We still rub shoulders outside the group regularly and stay in constant contact by phone. I'll often get a message from them to let me know what they are doing, often in reference to Cornerstone schools and the ministries in which we are mutually interested. These messages usually note that they are praying for me.

In our accountability group meetings, there's no set format. Often one of us will start off with comment on a passage from the Gospels that has struck home in the last several days. Then we will talk about mutual concerns.

We also "speak into each other's lives," as we call it, in fellowship as brothers. In our meetings, the three of us say what we've heard or seen about another's conduct that may not be honoring to God. "The way you are acting, you're sending a different message from what you intend," one of us may say. Or something more direct and candid—after twelve years of meeting together, we can be brutally honest. (I'd caution those starting an accountability group to proceed slowly in this regard. Trust has to be built up before a person can make use of such information.) I take

Between Two Worlds

the others' comments and pray over them, trying to understand what God wants to tell me through them. What God doesn't convict me about, I let go. What He does, I try to change as quickly as possible.

□ □ □

As I pursue these various spiritual disciplines, I try never to forget that it's all about God's love. I always remember the passage in John 15 where Jesus calls His disciples friends. Jesus has washed their feet, Judas has left the Upper Room, and in John's gospel, one can almost feel the tension go out of our Lord. In His last addresses to His disciples and His prayers for them to the Father, Jesus gets down to basics. Jesus is as open as He possibly can be, given the disciples' still limited understanding of His mission, and He draws them close to Him one final time in a new way:

> This is my commandment: love one another as I love you. No one has greater love than this, to lay down one's life for one's friends. You are my friends if you do what I command you. I no longer call you slaves, because a slave does not know what his master is doing. I have called you friends, because I have told you everything I have heard from my Father. (John 15:12-15)

I often think of Jesus' Passion as John narrates it, beginning with the agony in the garden. Jesus looks back toward Jerusalem and sees the torches of His betrayer and of the accompanying soldiers as they march through the Valley of Kidron toward Him. Peter, James, and John are asleep, as are the rest of the disciples. Jesus is already anticipating the physical punishment He knows

He'll endure—and worse, His separation from the Father.

I think about what Jesus must have gone through, seeing Judas coming toward Him, this man to whom He had given so much. What would I say in such a circumstance? "Judas, how could you do this to me?" Probably far worse. Yet Jesus reached out to him once more. He called him by the exact same name He has called the other disciples, "Friend." This teaches me that as a true follower of Jesus, I have no right to reject anyone. "Love your enemies," Jesus said, and He does so in that critical hour of human and divine history.

I focus on the incredible passion God has for me, once again calling John 17:23 to mind: "I in them [His disciples] and you [Father] in me," Jesus prays, "that they may be brought to perfection as one, that the world may know that you sent me, and that you loved them even as you loved me." The Father loves us, loves *me*, even as He loves the Son. That thought is so staggering that it's hard to fathom. When I accept it on faith, though, I begin to understand the passion God has for me. The only way I can get a handle on it is to think of the love I have for my grandchildren—the absolute love I have for them. I would gladly die for them. I would protect them at all costs, spending every last penny to help one that was sick. Even so, my love for my grandchildren pales in comparison to the incredible passion God has for me, as imperfect as I am. The infinite God who was all perfect became sin for me so that I might be His friend in this life and the next.

Because of God's great love, I've wanted to draw ever closer to Him through whatever gifts in prayer He thought best to grant. One of these is contemplation—a powerful and peaceful experience of God's presence. I recall the time I went with Doug and some companions to a Trappist retreat center in Spencer, Massachusetts. We heard a series of lectures on contemplation—or centering prayer, as many now call it—by an expert. I was excited about going deeper, about contemplation as an abandonment in Christ, and I prayed constantly during the retreat that I would be given this gift.

Our expert advised us to read *The Cloud of Unknowing*. Through the book and the lectures, we learned that often a single word or short phrase will trigger contemplation. I tried "Jesus," and "Trinity," and "Father," and "Come, Holy Spirit," but none of these words or phrases seemed to get me anywhere.

My entire time at the retreat had a comic aspect. I was having some dental work done around that time, and I had a temporary false tooth in front. During a break, my friends and I were sitting on a hillside, and I was chewing on a weed stem. My false tooth suddenly flew out of my mouth. For the rest of the retreat, I had a hole in my mouth you could park a Hummer in.

When I left the retreat, I still hadn't made any progress in prayer, and I felt a little depressed, what with the hole in my mouth and what seemed God's decision to withhold the gift of contemplation.

A couple of years went by, and one day I was praying after Mass. The church was empty except for me. I always ended my prayers in those days by saying, "God, You know I love You. I love You, Lord, with all my heart, soul, strength, and mind. Help me to love others through the love of You."

After I uttered those words, I heard a strong voice say, "Don't pray that." For a moment I thought I was under satanic attack—I really did. I felt like somebody had slapped me across the face. I remember thinking, *What do you mean, don't pray that? That's the Great Commandment.*

The next words I heard were, "You're too imperfect. You don't love Me with all your heart, with all your soul, with all your mind, with all your strength. You're just too imperfect."

Tears came into my eyes, and I said, "I'm trying, God. I want to."

I sat there absolutely stunned and thought, *Is this of God? Is God telling me this?*

Suddenly, I realized what I was being told was true. I was so imperfect there wasn't any way I could love God with all my heart, soul, mind, and strength.

Then God said something: "Your word is *yield*. Why don't you pray that you will yield to Me? Why don't you yield your heart to My heart so that you have My purity of heart? Why don't you yield your soul to My soul so that you're one with Me in the Father and Holy Spirit? Why don't you yield your mind to My mind so that you begin to think and talk and act like Me? And why don't you yield your strength to My strength, because My strength will give you the strength for everything."

I heard this word for word, just as I've written it here. I realized I had crossed another threshold in my relationship with God. Now, every day, I pray as God instructed me. My process of sanctification is to yield myself to God in every area of my life.

I find that often after I pray this prayer, I feel the presence of God directly. The only thing I can compare the experience to is my marriage. Nancy and I can sit on the couch and look at each other and contemplate our love for each other. We don't have to talk, I can look at her, she can look at me, and we can speak volumes in a glance. I'm aware not only of her physical presence, but of her soul as well. The experience of contemplative prayer is like that. The feeling is an overwhelming sense of God's presence and peace, of His nearness, of feeling His love for me and my love for Him and our communion.

My communication with God has to be ongoing and becomes

as entangled as anyone else's in the day's cares. I normally take the dog out for a walk at about eleven each night, and while I do I breathe out a few prayers to God, summing up my day, talking things over with Him—asking God to take care of what I can only leave in His hands. Usually, I tell Him a long list of the things I'm worried about.

At these times, I often hear God say, "Why don't you just be quiet? Why don't you just rest in Me?"

Chapter Thirteen

Avoiding the Snares

When Michael reached Uganda in the fall of 1988, the cushy life he had imagined—living in a lakeside house, riding horses, trolling Lake Victoria—quickly vanished. His African host, the amazing entrepreneur Gordon Wavamunno, took care of him well enough. He was given a bedroom in Gordon's home on his gated property at the outskirts of Kampala and an Audi to drive. As to the lakeside mansion, though, only the foundation had been poured. There was a boat, but it sat half-submerged two hundred yards offshore. The one horse Gordon owned was stabled at a neighboring farm. It suffered from mange and had gone entirely bald. It was a pink, slouch-backed skeleton on hooves. Within a week, the beast died.

These disappointments might have rattled Michael prior to his conversion. He recognized now that being away from his old haunts and friends was what he needed. Gordon also supplied him with an office at his downtown building. "I don't care what you do," I told Michael before he left. "Just do it from nine to five."

Like many serious converts, including St. Paul after his Damascus road experience, Michael spent the next season of his life in spiritual training. He read the Bible for eight hours a day for months. He read a few works of theology as well, but mainly he read the Scriptures, multiple books at a sitting, relying on the Holy Spirit as his teacher.

Michael also threw himself into Ugandan life, attending a Pentecostal church at first, but returning to his roots by embracing Catholicism, even becoming a daily communicant. He quickly came to love the Ugandan people, although he found a society torn asunder by twenty-five years of government-sponsored oppression and cruelty.

After Uganda gained independence in 1962, the country suffered under the regimes of Milton Obote and the infamous Idi Amin. Two years before Michael arrived, President Yoweri Museveni had come to power, and he was restoring stability to the country, slowly introducing democratic reforms and encouraging a free press.[18] As a result of the brutal dictatorships of Obote and Amin, there were thousands upon thousands of orphans in Uganda. The shops thronged with "market boys," teenagers who worked as freelance gofers, helping to negotiate purchases, carrying sacks, and so forth. The AIDS epidemic was beginning to hit as well, leaving orphaned children by the thousands.

It had been Michael's intention to engage in humanitarian work even before his conversion. He now saw the tragic need of Uganda's orphans. He began in small ways, making inquiries among local agencies and giving assistance where possible.

Michael became acquainted with some poor people on the streets as well as some powerful individuals. He met President Yoweri Museveni, cabinet officials, and many representatives in the newly formed parliament. I was then traveling on behalf of The Fellowship, meeting with government leaders in different parts of the world. Over the next few years, Michael traveled with me from time to time, and he caught the vision of what could be done for the poor by presenting Jesus to leaders.

Michael and Gordon came up with the idea of building a hospital in President Yoweri's hometown, Rushere. No hospital had been built in Uganda since independence in 1962. A quarter of a million people lived in Rushere, and there was then no central medical facility. A number of businessmen promised to join the effort, and the president's personal physician promised to recruit the staff.

When it came time to build the hospital, Michael provided the project's leadership. Though only twenty-four years old, he took it upon himself to serve as the hospital's general contractor. Logistics presented the greatest challenges. There were no supplies to speak of in Rushere—concrete, bricks, rebar, and everything else had to be trucked in.

Michael found a tough but reliable Ugandan named Charles to supervise the workers, who lived in tents onsite. Michael rented a huge truck and kept it running nearly night and day, bringing in building materials. He kept everyone motivated by adopting the landowner's method from Jesus' parable: He would show up at any time, though no one knew when. Sometimes he would drive the four hours from Kampala to Rushere for a short, unexpected visit, then turn around and drive straight back again. Spurred on by the boss's check-ins, the workers completed their tasks, and the hospital opened in 1992. It included about sixty beds, a minor operating theater, an outpatient clinic, and a pharmacy. The president's physician followed through and found qualified people to staff the facility.

I'll never forget arriving to tour the hospital soon after it opened. A Ugandan man met Michael, Nancy, and me outside. He claimed he was the project's leader—even though Michael had never seen him before—and proceeded to give us a grand tour. With amused humility, my son let our "guide" go on and on about the place.

Afterward, Michael and I had a talk that was a turning point in our relationship. I let him know that if he never did another thing in his life, he was a man in my eyes. In my youth, I had aspired to be a builder of society and succeeded, but I had never done anything like build a hospital in an African nation. In comparison to Michael's achievement, what I had done was routine. And my son hadn't yet reached thirty.

Michael went on to found a ministry known as Cornerstone Development. (Michael's Cornerstone preceded the cluster of schools named Cornerstone in Detroit.) After the hospital came several other ministries, chief among them a high school named Cornerstone Leadership Academy. The academy actually serves as a bridge from high school to university. It takes students after they have completed their "O levels," the first round of secondary exams in the British system. Cornerstone prepares these students to take their more advanced exams, or "A levels," which qualify them for university studies.

At the time, Michael was working with two colleagues, Tim Kreutter and John Riordan. These three young men saw that an advanced high school might prepare a whole new generation of Ugandan leaders. They saw that the real problem in the Third World (or Global South) wasn't lack of financing but lack of leadership. Through our travels together, Michael had seen that by the time most African leaders ascend to power, they have made so many compromises that expecting justice from them can be a frail hope. The young leaders of Cornerstone Development saw that it would be much easier to form a new generation of African leaders than to persuade the present leaders to reform. Thus Cornerstone Leadership Academy was founded and operates today as a dynamic institution of intellectual and spiritual formation. Its guiding principle is, "Love God with all your heart, soul, strength and mind, and love one another for the love of Him."

Michael's Cornerstone Development efforts helped form our thinking about our family foundation's philosophy. We had established this foundation around the time of my work in Peru and other Latin American countries, and it gained momentum through Michael's work in Uganda. He saw that there tended to be a strict division between missionaries who were interested in peoples' souls and development workers whose concerns were economic. Cornerstone Development embraced what might be called a philosophy of "spiritual investment." It addressed both the earthly and spiritual concerns of the academy's students. It leveraged the monies allocated by helping to form leaders who would, in turn, go on to provide for others' earthly and spiritual needs, as government and business leaders and as Christ-centered men. The effects of Cornerstone have been rippling throughout Ugandan society for well over a decade. Today we have four Cornerstone schools in Uganda. We have now also opened a Cornerstone school in Rwanda, as well as a number of homes for street children and other programs for kids, with plans to open more Cornerstone schools in neighboring countries.

□ □ □

During the course of Michael's years in Uganda, I saw him mature as a follower of Jesus. He went from being self-absorbed to living to serve others. He took on organizational challenges for which there were few precedents. Happily, in the midst of the work, Michael found time to return to the States occasionally, where he met and eventually married a young woman from our Grosse

Pointe community, Laura Gagnon. God gave us another Laura, and through this wonderful young couple, four grandchildren.

Michael and Laura moved back to the States in 1996, and they both entered and completed the University of Michigan's MBA program. Now Michael works with our family foundation and as a business coach. He helps supervise the ongoing work of Cornerstone Development and many other projects. His practical experience in Uganda, his advanced training in business administration, and his heart for the Lord give him tremendous insight into how the family foundation can best allocate its resources.

Michael's growth made me so thankful for how Christ brings out the image of God in each of us. Spiritual maturity leads to the practice of virtue and charity. This has a redemptive effect not only on individuals but also on the lives of their family, their community, and their country. God's love redeems us, makes us who we truly are as men and women. We, in turn, are called to be witnesses to this transformation and to help create outposts of the kingdom of God in the midst of a fallen world. God's redemptive work in our lives compels us to build a livable community for believers and nonbelievers alike.

□ □ □

My own journey, and my relationship with Michael, prepared me to be involved with the Promise Keepers organization. There was and is a huge hunger for American men to become people of God, and the astounding growth of this evangelical men's movement testified that it had struck a chord in many hearts.

Founded in 1990 by University of Colorado coach Bill McCartney and Dr. Dave Wardell, Promise Keepers filled CU's stadium, Folsom Field, with fifty thousand men within three years of its launch. Promise Keepers quickly became known for its stadium events, featuring some of the best Christian speakers in the country, and its energizing, contemporary worship songs. In 1996, Promise Keepers drew more than a million men to twenty-two nationwide events. The next year an estimated one million gathered on the National Mall in Washington, DC, to pray, confess, repent of their sins, and declare their intention to keep their faith in God and their godly promises to their loved ones.

Promise Keepers asks conference participants to commit themselves to seven promises, the first of which is to honor Jesus Christ through worship, prayer, and obedience to God's Word. The second promise involves a commitment to meet with other like-minded men as a means of strengthening their spiritual life and moral resolve. Prior to coming to Colorado, McCartney had been an assistant coach at the University of Michigan, where he benefited from the Word of God Community—a Catholic and ecumenical group devoted to renewal. The program of Promise Keepers reflected what he had learned there about the importance of discipleship and spiritual formation.

I understood, of course, from my own experience how worthwhile accountability groups are. The rest of the Promise Keepers program also synchronized with my personal experience. I had already followed God's leading in building a stronger marriage, as Promise Keepers asks of men. The organization also asks men to support their local church and reach beyond denominational and racial barriers to fellow Christians and non-Christians. Promise Keepers foresaw millions seeking to influence the world through obedience to the Great Commandment and the Great Commission. These were already my own desires, so I had a ready heart for the work of Promise Keepers and the task of evangelizing men.

My first encounters with the ministry were powerful as well. I went to a stadium event where seventy-five thousand men joined hands and sang the Lord's Prayer together. That was one of the greatest experiences I can imagine this side of heaven. Promise Keepers proved what the Catholic renewal leader Ralph Martin says (paraphrasing John 12:32): "Wherever you lift up Jesus, men will go." Millions of men saw Jesus presented clearly through Promise Keepers.

In seeing Jesus, we also come to understand who we are meant to be as Christian men. Our identity has been particularly difficult to understand since the sexual revolution of the 1960s. Since that time, popular culture has seen men as either unattached, free-wheeling playboys—really, adolescents with big bank accounts—or nincompoop husbands. The old TV show celebrated that "father knows best," but since that time "father" has been a dimwit—good for nothing other than being the butt of the joke. The media have consistently portrayed men as irrelevant.

Promise Keepers began talking about what it really means to be a man. The ministry pointed out that God calls men into a biblical role: Men are to be the spiritual leaders of their families. This does not diminish or demean the woman's role. It lifts up, protects, and celebrates the role a woman plays in nurturing her household. The spiritual authority that men exercise demands that they serve their families as Christ served the church—a truly daunting example of sacrificial leadership. The true challenge of a man's life is to pour out his life for his family, which demands more courage, fidelity, and perseverance than any rebel without a cause has ever mustered. Biblical manhood represents a challenge that can be accomplished only by God's grace. Promise Keepers told men forthrightly that when they shirked the challenges of

biblical manhood—including moral, ethical, and sexual purity—they weren't really being men.

Promise Keepers dealt with pornography, substance and alcohol abuse, gambling, unethical business dealings—many issues
that weren't being talked about elsewhere. Promise Keepers said
clearly, "You cannot be a man and do these things." Your number-
one calling is to lift your wife up to Jesus Christ, to love your
wife as Christ loved the church. To me, Promise Keepers took the
most pro-woman stance imaginable. As a woman friend of mine
says, "The true solution for so many 'women's problems' is for
men to be *better*."

Of course, feminists often view Promise Keepers with suspi-
cion and hostility, finding any discussion of a man's leadership
within the family threatening. But Promise Keepers did a smart
thing and opened itself to any woman who wanted to attend and
observe what was being said and done. Women could and did dis-
agree with Promise Keepers' point of view, but few walked away
without some admiration for its call to responsibility.

□ □ □

One day, Peb Jackson, whom I knew through The Fellowship and
who was then head of development for Young Life, called and
asked if I would join the board of Promise Keepers. "We know
you're a committed Catholic," Peb said, "and we're serious as an
organization about Promise Keepers keeping the sixth promise:
'to reach beyond any racial and denominational barriers to demonstrate the power of biblical unity.'"

I said that I would pray about the matter and attend a board
meeting as a means of discerning the Lord's leading. Soon after, I
agreed to join the board.

The other Promise Keepers board members were friendly and warm. At the same time, I was always aware of being the lone Catholic representative. The organization remained wary about mentioning Catholic participation at its events. Ralph Martin and I, as well as other Catholics, spoke at Promise Keepers events, but our suggestion that Promise Keepers invite Catholic clergy to speak was repeatedly put off.

So there came a time when I felt I should leave the board of Promise Keepers due to my growing responsibility with Prison Fellowship International and my desire to reach out to Catholic men in a context that they would understand.

□ □ □

Promise Keepers recognized a hunger among Catholic men, particularly in the northern cities, where Catholics constituted a significant percentage of Promise Keepers attendees. In fact, the United State Conference of Catholic Bishops prepared a largely favorable report on Promise Keepers in June 1996. The report said, "PK is the proverbial wake-up call to the Church to encourage and offer more ministry suited to the needs of men." It advised the Catholic clergy and laity to take a proactive position in responding to men's spiritual issues. "Let us focus and expend our energies on what we can offer distinctively from within the Roman Catholic tradition."[19]

Kevin Lynch, founder of Catholic Men's Fellowship of Greater Cincinnati, did just that by establishing a yearly Answer the Call conference in 1995. The first conference drew more than 450 men to St. Gertrude's parish hall. Archbishop Pilarczyk celebrated Mass. Now thousands of men attend the yearly conference.

The Cincinnati conference and conferences in the New York

area and California, under the direction of Jim Manhardt, founder and president of Catholic Men for Jesus, prompted a group of twenty leaders in men's evangelism to meet with the United States Conference of Catholic Bishops' Committee on Marriage and Family and the Committee on Evangelism in September 1998. If there was to be a Catholic men's movement, we wanted it to function in concert with the hierarchy.

For the movement to continue, we needed a national clearinghouse providing support and teaching materials to local ministries. That came about in March of 2001 with the hiring of Maurice Blumberg as executive director of the organization now known as the National Fellowship of Catholic Men. The first board consisted of Father Phillip Merdinger from Boston, former pro football player Danny Abramowicz from New Orleans, Kevin Lynch, Jim Manhardt, former U.S. Senator Jeremiah Denton, and me.

From the beginning, the United States Conference of Catholic Bishops has been enthusiastic in its support. Cardinal Maida serves as the organization's ecclesial adviser. As a result of God's grace and this coordinated effort, the National Fellowship of Catholic Men has grown tremendously. In 2005, thirty events attracted more than forty thousand men. In 2006 and 2007, we held over forty events throughout the United States.

The Catholic men's movement works not only through large, arena-filling conferences but — even more importantly — through parish groups. These give men the opportunity to talk and pray about the issues that matter to them, in a setting where they feel at ease. Most women prefer to talk with other women about relationships, family, children, and job responsibilities. Similarly, most men won't talk honestly about their Big Three issues — money, sex, and power — except in the company of other men.

□ □ □

When I speak to men's groups, large and small, I share my own experience with the Big Three as a means of encouraging hard thinking and even harder prayer. The issue of money is often more corrosive in a marriage than sex. Our culture tells us that we shouldn't delay satisfying our desires; instant gratification has become our way of life. As much as we try to fight this as followers of Jesus, we find it hard to resist the attitude of entitlement: "I work hard—I deserve this." There's also a tremendous compulsion in our world to acquire status through things. For example, a new car gives us bragging rights. Many of the forces that make handling money difficult are right out in the open—on every billboard and in every television ad.

But there are deeper motivations that make handling money particularly difficult for men. I was blessed with a wife who was willing to scrimp and save. We bought secondhand furniture—some of which we still have—and we borrowed only for our first, small mortgage. Still, until I was about thirty-five, I had feelings of insecurity as a provider. Nearly every man wants to fulfill his obligations to his family. Some of the strangest things men do—their secrecy, angry silences, and catastrophic financial decisions—are attributable not to irresponsibility, but to being overwhelmed by their desire to be responsible.

Recently, I was speaking with a man in his early forties whose story illustrates this. His company was moving out of state, and so he had lost his job. Because he had been coming to talk with me for a while, he knew he could trust me with this information. He was incredibly embarrassed, and I could see his self-esteem was in tatters. He was a sharp and talented young businessman, but he had still lost his job.

As we talked, he said, "My marriage is affected, and I'm afraid my wife doesn't have the same esteem for me as she used to."

I was kind of shocked.

"We don't talk about it," he said, "but I can see how she looks at me when I have nothing to do but hang around the house."

I told him, "You know, friend, *that's* the problem—you're not talking about it. Go home and share what's on your heart. You are a provider, and you will provide. But if you allow the silence to continue, then even when you find a new job, as I'm sure you will, this issue will lurk in the background. You'll ask yourself, *Is there a wound in my marriage? Does she really trust me?* You have to deal with this *now*."

He took my advice. We talked on the phone a short while after, and he was feeling more confident. Ultimately, he did find a new position, and he could see how the struggle had been beneficial to his marriage.

I have a friend named Tony who prays about every major decision in his life, including purchases. He's a man with the courage to ask Christ, "Shall I buy this house? Do I need this car?" He looks to me as his spiritual mentor, and we talk over these questions as well. I always tell him, "Whatever I tell you, take it to God in prayer. Whatever I say is only my opinion. It may be true or partially true or, for you, not true. But if you sincerely take it to God, He will lead you. He is faithful."

God answers our questions in one of three ways. He says "yes," "no," or "wait." As Americans, we like "yes" answers and can even deal with "no" answers. But being told to wait is particularly tough. In waiting, we're submitting to His control. Often we must wait and discern His will through prayer, as Jesus discerned the will of His Father. The Holy Spirit inspired the writers of the Passion accounts to demonstrate that even Jesus, in His human character, had difficulties. In the Garden of Gethsemane, He faced what He had to do, but as a man He didn't want to suffer.

But ultimately Jesus submitted to the will of the Father.

That gives me incredible insight into my own life and the strength of leaning on God. There are many things I don't want to do, and there are things I'm scared to death can happen. But if I submit to the will of God, He is with me, and glorious things will result.

□ □ □

The next big issue I talk to men about is sex. C. S. Lewis points out that while lust and gluttony are both sins, no one goes to a bar to ogle a beef Wellington as men do with strippers. The temptation of illicit sex often seems far more difficult to resist than other temptations.

Even though I'm in my sixties, I experience as much temptation as I did in my twenties. When men start fantasizing about a woman, they often become obsessive. Chuck Swindoll said something years ago that I often repeat to men and for my own benefit as well: "Adultery occurs in the head long before it occurs in bed."

In my case, I had reached a point where I thought my prayer disciplines had made me immune to sexual temptation. I felt relieved. "Gee, I'm beyond this." Then one of my partners in the law firm hired an absolutely beautiful young woman who dressed in a way that accentuated her figure. I worked closely with this partner and was constantly going into his office, where I would see her. I quickly realized that I could become obsessed with her. From the beginning, I prayed about what I should do, and I found the answer in "avoiding the occasion of sin." I stopped going to my partner's office and instead had him come to mine. I committed to the Lord that I would not think about her. After a while, the temptation passed, and I felt zero attraction.

In retrospect, I recognize that I had become presumptuous, thinking I was beyond sin. The Lord allowed me to be tempted as a lesson. He allowed me to see that if I reject Him or neglect Him, there isn't anything that I'm not capable of, including adultery, although I love my wife with all my heart.

Disciplined habits are the key to fighting what has been called "every man's battle." We all have our times of temptation, and usually we know what they are. Many men—and women for that matter—whose work involves travel find being on the road a time of testing. We feel displaced, lonely, and those we're accountable to are far away.

I set a discipline early on when I started traveling for business. As often as I can, I go with someone else. In the days when Talon was getting started, Randy and I often traveled together and played gin rummy to keep ourselves occupied during downtimes.

When I travel alone, I don't drink, and I normally don't eat alone in restaurants. I have room service. I'm not going to go have a drink in the bar and sit there and talk to somebody, because I know that's a recipe for disaster. Even when a man eats alone in a restaurant, his mind can wander and become preoccupied with good-looking women. I don't care how old someone is, there is temptation. I've known of men in their seventies getting ensnared in adulterous affairs that tear their families apart.

Most occasions of temptation can be countered with disciplined habits. Ultimately, these disciplines find their motivation in Jesus' passionate love for us and our continuing acknowledgment of His presence in prayer. When we remain in conversation with God, we aren't going to say, "Excuse me, Jesus, I've got to go commit adultery now," just as we'd never stop in the middle of dinner in a restaurant with our wives to say, "Excuse me, honey, but I'm attracted to that woman over there."

The analogy between what we would do when in the company of our wives or husbands and what we are likely to do when remaining faithful in prayer comes from the heart of what marriage is meant to be—a school in how to love. God has given us marriage to understand the exclusive love relationship between God and humankind.

□ □ □

The most corrupting temptation of all must be power. We tend to think of political power in regard to this issue. But there are struggles for power in marriages and every other type of relationship, where one person tries to gain exclusive control. Many of us, whether we work in an office or a factory, exercise some degree of control over other people and find ourselves desiring power either to escape economic or relational burdens or for the sheer pleasure of wielding it, which gratifies our ego.

I remember meeting with the leader of an African nation, a true despot. His government was corrupt. The security police regularly targeted his enemies and put people to death. That man seemed absolutely cold, and he had almost no range of positive emotion. He looked as if he had never had a happy day in his life, because he was obsessed with not losing his power. He was the most powerful man in his country, and yet he lived in an imprisoning fear worse than his dungeons.

I remember how fatiguing it was to try to impose my will on others. It was also self-depreciating. I would get so upset at times that I would walk out of a meeting sick to my stomach and hating myself for it. Heeding God's call, on the other hand, is liberating. Work becomes a matter of obedience, not control or manipulation.

I can respond as God directs and leave the outcome of my actions in His hands.

Jesus is the perfect model for this, of course. He says, "A son cannot do anything on his own, but only what he sees his father doing; for what he does, his son will do also. For the Father loves his Son and shows him everything that he himself does" (John 5:19-20). If Jesus lived His life in obedience, even "becoming obedient to death" (Philippians 2:8), how can I expect to find fulfillment except by doing the same?

As a result of accepting this truth, I'm able to deal with many complex and even emotionally difficult situations far more effectively. The authority I feel now is stronger because I know it's not of me, it's God-given. I stay in communication with God to have this assurance, and I constantly ask Him, "Is this something You want me to do?"

Understanding God's call on our lives leads us to understand the true nature of leadership, which is servanthood—the second means of exercising power. Those in a position of influence over others have to look at power as a God-given responsibility and trust. If someone desires to be a leader, he or she never will be (though he or she may hold some position of authority). True leaders sublimate their ego to a larger purpose. If someone wants to lead, as the Scriptures teach, that person will become a servant. Those who go out and serve, who are compassionate and kind, are the people we look up to. Intimidation isn't leadership; it's manipulation.

The quest for power must give way to the quest for perfection in love. If you said to me, "If you died tomorrow, what would you like people to say about you?" my answer would be, "Mike loved the people God gave him, and he was a good man." That would be thrilling, because that's exactly what Scripture tells us to desire; it is a paraphrase of what God will say to the just: "Well done, my good and faithful servant" (Matthew 25:23). That is my goal in life—to be good and faithful.

□ □ □

The hunger of men to gather together and talk about issues comes most of all, I believe, from the inability of so many fathers and sons to connect. Once after I spoke at Franciscan University in Steubenville, I decided to spend the afternoon in the chapel. I had felt the presence of God while I spoke, and I wanted to reflect on what I'd heard as people greeted me afterward. I was lost in my thoughts, my heart full of gratitude, half kneeling, half sitting in a pew. Suddenly, someone tapped me on the shoulder. It was a big, burly guy, heavily tattooed. "Mr. Timmis, can I talk to you?" he asked.

"Sure," I said. "Do you have a problem?"

"No, no problem, but I wanted to thank you."

"Thank me for what?"

"Well, I was here last year," he explained. "As you ended your talk, you said, 'If you've come here this weekend and you don't resolve to heal your relationship either with your son or with your father, depending on where the brokenness is, then you've wasted your time here. And you'll get nothing out of this unless you deal with this issue, because it's an impediment to growth in God.'"

I often say this, and the response has been and continues to be overwhelming.

This young man said, "I'd like you to know that I left here and I drove eight hundred miles straight to my father. I asked his forgiveness."

Thank you, God, I thought. *Thank you for him and for me.* "I appreciate that," I said. "That's really an encouragement."

I went back to my prayers for about forty-five minutes. When I was walking out of the chapel, I saw this young man again. He was standing with his father, who was dressed in a light-blue blazer with a white button-down shirt and khaki slacks. From their radically different styles of dress, I guessed that they had endured many battles.

The father came up to me and said, "Mr. Timmis, I want to thank you, and I want you to know that my son and I are growing together in Jesus."

I've been given many gifts, but there's no gift that can surpass that. When I return home after speaking engagements, I love sharing stories like this with Nancy, because she makes our witness possible. If it weren't for her steady presence at home, I could never go where I feel called. When we reflect on experiences like the reconciliation between this father and son, we understand how the Lord is using us, and we are grateful.

☐ ☐ ☐

Not long after my own spiritual reawakening, I had my own reckoning with my dad. He was in his eighties and had undergone hip replacement surgery. It wasn't a good idea for him to drive any longer, so my brothers and I bought him a house in an area close to where my brothers and sisters live. He had to give up the farm in north Michigan that he loved, along with his horses, and I know that was difficult for him.

My siblings and I would alternate taking my dad and stepmother out on Saturday night to dinner. On one of these occasions, not long after I had become a serious follower of Jesus, my dad asked, "What's happened to you?"

"What do you mean?" I replied.

"Son, you're different. You've changed."

"Dad, I've asked Jesus into my life," I told him. "I've really committed myself."

He said gruffly, "What do you mean? You've always believed in Jesus."

"Yes, I know, Dad, but now it's different."

He began to get angry with me, questioning how I could think like that.

"Dad, could we just go home and talk about this?" I asked. "This is not the place to get into it."

"Well," he pressed on, "you didn't become one of those born-againers, did you?"

"You don't understand," I replied. "Let's just go home and talk there."

So we drove home. There I tried again to explain what had happened. "I'm forty-three years old, and we have never had a talk about anything other than sports," I said. "Please let me tell you what's on my heart." I started sharing my story, and before too long he started to weep. Nancy was sitting there too, and she was crying, as was my stepmother.

"Dad, can you understand now what's happened to me?" I asked.

He said, "Mike, I prayed all your life that you would come to know Jesus in just the way you told me."

What healing that conversation brought to our relationship! After that night, we began to speak about following Jesus. I asked him if he'd like to read the Bible with me.

"You know, I always wanted to read the Bible, but I didn't know how," he answered.

I said, "I'll get you a Bible."

He lived about forty-five minutes from us, so we'd often have a little Bible study by telephone. I'd suggest he read a certain passage, and then we'd call and discuss it. Those were some of our best times as father and son.

He and I were the same people, only now we could see into each other's hearts as never before. I'm glad to say that before he died I came to appreciate him in a whole new way.

It was only after he died, though, that I fully realized what he meant when he said that he had prayed all his life for me to know Jesus in a personal, intimate way. One day, not long after my father's passing in 1987, I was jogging and thanking God for my parents. I saw my father, as I used to see him when I was a child, rise up from the dinner table and go into his bedroom, where he would kneel down beside the bed. Life continued to swirl around with the kids and homework and talking on the phone in our three-bedroom bungalow house, but Dad would be kneeling by his bedside. I realized suddenly with a conviction brought by the Spirit that my dad had been praying for me—every night, night after night, in my childhood.

The protection I had always experienced had come through my father's and mother's prayers. Just before her death, as I shared earlier, my mother held up the crucifix to me, the sum of everything she wanted me to know. Similarly, my dad had lifted me up to the Lord in his nightly prayers. We are all so much more the product of God's graces—and our parents' abiding, if sometimes imperfect, love—than we ever suspect.

Chapter Fourteen

Setting the Captives — and the Church — Free

My relationship with Chuck Colson, founder of Prison Fellowship, began long before I met him. I remember hearing of his conversion in the post-Watergate period and thinking, as so many did, that he must be using religion to get himself off the hook. Later I was in the throes of my own spiritual wrestling when a friend gave me Chuck's landmark book, *Born Again*. How I wish now that I had read it promptly, instead of putting it aside.

After my own conversion experience, I met Chuck at an Executive Ministries dinner given at Nancy DeMoss's house outside Philadelphia. By then I understood how God can change people. I liked Chuck immediately, and within the span of a short conversation, we formed a bond. His drive and energy came through, as did his delight in others' gifts and activities. I could see Chuck getting fired up about my own experience and the steps I had taken to evangelize.

Over the next several years, particularly when I commuted to Washington to meet with Doug, I would see Chuck. He was always enthusiastic in his greeting and wanted to know what I had been doing. Before long, he extended an invitation to join the board of Prison Fellowship in the United States (PF USA). The invitation came days before Laura's death, though, and he understood when I called to decline.

In 1990, Nancy and I were at our winter house on Sanibel Island when Chuck telephoned again. He asked if he and his wife, Patty, could meet us for lunch. We gladly agreed and set a date.

Over lunch, Chuck asked a penetrating question: "What's God's call in your life, Mike?"

"To evangelize the poor," I said. "I believe what Doug Coe says is true, that if you can change a leader's heart, you can really help the poor. As you know, I've been traveling with Doug and others to meet with foreign leaders. I'll probably be doing that the rest of my life."

Chuck then asked a difficult question: "Mike, who do you think is the poorest of the poor?"

At that point, I had traveled extensively throughout the Third World. "I don't know, Chuck," I said. "I've seen a lot of poverty."

"I would like you to think about this," Chuck said. "The poorest of the poor are prisoners and their families, because they've had everything taken away from them, including their dignity. Even their names, in most cases."

I had never thought about prisoners in this light. "I see your point," I said. I saw as well that Chuck was recruiting me once more for PF USA's board. I was unsure of whether to go forward. Prison ministry seemed too narrowly focused. So I told him, "I don't know if I'm called to work with only one element among the poor. I want to be with all of the poor in lots of different contexts."

"There's one other thing you need to understand," he said. "I've heard about your talks on the unity within the body of Christ—the fellowship of all true followers of Jesus, whether evangelicals, Catholics, or Orthodox. I am writing a book called *The Body*. It's a call to evangelicals and Catholics to meet together in the person of Jesus Christ. It shows how we need to stand together in this time of cultural crisis. What unites us is so much greater than what divides us."

I certainly agreed with that.

He went on. "You've been in the evangelical world, and you're familiar with it, but you've remained a committed Catholic."

"More committed now than ever," I said.

"Right," he continued. "What would we say to the world if we stood together as brothers and proclaimed the truth of our unity in Jesus?"

My defenses collapsed. "That really tugs at my heart," I said, "because I know there's no hope unless we do that."

I believe, as Chuck believes, that the problem in the world is that we call ourselves Christians, but we don't act like Jesus. No one can blame those who don't know Jesus for not acting like Him. But those of us who do know the Lord and do not act together in a spirit of love are indeed blameworthy. As Chuck said that day, the only hope we have of fighting our enemy Satan and the sin of division that the Evil One wants to engender is through uniting in our common Lord—in the person of Jesus Christ. When we do that, our theological differences become secondary. As followers of Jesus Christ we can work together across every theological divide to act as the body of Christ and show the world Christ's love.

So I told Chuck I would join PF USA's board. His call to unity made the difference for me. I was not sure how involved I would ever become in prison ministry itself, though. I thought I could probably help PF USA mostly in its administration.

My experience of prison ministry soon became personal, as a

member of my accountability group, Chuck McLeod, suggested I meet a prisoner he had been counseling. That seemed only right. Because I was serving on the board, I should become personally involved in prison ministry.

The prisoner I came to know—whom I'll call Sandy—had a colorful story. Sandy was the son of a corrections officer—the rebellious child in a family with eight children. He became involved in drugs and began dealing. Just before Sandy was caught by the police, he became a believer, but he decided to follow through on a previously arranged deal, succumbing to the temptation of one last score. That landed him in prison for longer than he ever could have imagined.

Michigan had a law stipulating that anyone caught with a certain amount of narcotics with intent to distribute had to serve a mandatory twenty-year prison sentence with no possibility of parole. Sandy had no prior convictions and no history of violence, but he was found in possession of a sufficient amount of narcotics to mandate a twenty-year sentence. His lawyer must have been both incompetent and greedy, because he pled Sandy to twenty years with no parole and charged the family twenty-five thousand dollars for his trouble.

When I met Sandy, he had already served seven years. He was full of the love of the Lord, which was, of course, a good thing. This led to writing his favorite Christian leaders to solicit their help, an endeavor that backfired. He wrote Chuck Colson, Bill McCartney, James Dobson, and probably Billy Graham as well. More than one Christian leader responded to his entreaties, and this made the prison officials absolutely determined not to cut Sandy any slack; they didn't want to be accused of religious bias—or gullibility.

I knew Michigan's governor at the time, John Engler. He had

twisted my arm to serve as regent of Wayne State University, an appointment that required reviewing a four-inch-high stack of documents every month. I served for six years and was glad I did, because the board truly had a significant role in the institution's governance.

I called Governor Engler about Sandy's situation and thousands like him. I pointed out the economic disaster Sandy's incarceration was for the state, potentially costing over a million dollars. After that long in prison, Sandy would probably be on welfare for the rest of his life—few employers would want to hire someone who had done a twenty-year stretch. "It's just absolutely crazy," I told him, "to keep someone in prison for that long, with no prior offenses and no history of violence."

After the Willie Horton story torpedoed Michael Dukakis's run for president, no politician in the country would let someone out of prison early who might commit another offense. Engler saw the logic of what I was saying, but he thought it unwise to commute Sandy's sentence. He intended to work more broadly on reforming the whole concept of mandatory minimums. Even so, I kept bringing up Sandy's situation to the governor whenever I had the chance.

A few weeks before Engler left office, I received a call from his chief legal officer. "Mike, the governor wants you to know that you've lost the battle, but you've won the war."

"What does that mean?" I asked.

"He's not going to commute the sentence of your friend."

"Oh," I said, "I'm sorry to hear that."

"But as one of his last acts in office, he's having a bill passed in the Senate and the House eliminating the law," he explained. "He agrees that it's stupid to spend huge amounts of money keeping people in prison when they are no threat to the community."

This meant that Sandy's sentence could be reviewed by a parole board. That's what happened, and after serving eleven years, he was finally released.

Once a free man again, Sandy began working for his cousin, doing odd jobs. I had spoken to him previously about hiring him, thinking I'd find something for him in one of Talon's businesses. As it turned out, our family needed a caretaker, and I offered Sandy the position. He accepted and came to work for us.

Through our relationship, I saw up close the difficulties a former prisoner has adjusting to life on the outside. Like many prisoners, Sandy was incarcerated at a young age — as he was just emerging into manhood. Men like Sandy go from what they've known of a home life to institutional life, where every decision is made for them. Because he never had to cope with the usual ups and downs of life on his own, his coping skills were meager upon his release. The usual bumps in the road could throw him for a loop. All along the way, he's continued to adjust and improve, but it's been hard.

Sandy worked for us for two years. He took a home inspection course and now has his own company and is married. His future looks bright. Sandy opened my eyes, though, to how difficult life is for prisoners who are simply thrown back onto the streets.

I saw the wisdom in PF USA's deep belief in "restorative justice." For nonviolent offenders — and I want to stress that violent criminals must be handled differently — PF USA believes in minimal jail time. It also believes that nonviolent offenders ought to make restitution to their victims, paying back whatever money might have been stolen or performing work as compensation of other losses. The ministry also believes that prisoners need to be reestablished in the community through Christ-centered outreach. As I saw with Sandy, in most cases this means the offender needs to be *established* in a real community, since so many prisoners know nothing but the streets and their criminal elements. Offenders need to be invited to accept Jesus Christ as their personal Savior. They also need to be surrounded by a loving church community and given tutoring, job skills, and spiritual and psychological counseling through their close network of peers and mentors.

This may sound like a giant giveaway program, with potentially dangerous consequences, but actually it is much less expensive than locking people up and then releasing them to commit more crimes before locking them up again. The United States has 2.3 million people in prison right now, and it costs on average twenty to thirty-five thousand dollars per year to keep someone incarcerated. That figure includes only living costs. It doesn't include the massive sums spent as we build ever more prisons. Restorative justice provides for victims' rights — which a merely punitive approach does not — and also values the image of God in which everyone is made. As I've come to know more and more prisoners, I've realized that under particular circumstances, I might have committed nearly every offense my prisoner friends have committed. We are all sinners and fall short of the glory of God.

□ □ □

In November of 1997, I came in from a cold Detroit day to my law office. Chuck was calling from Paris. "We've just had a board meeting of Prison Fellowship International," he told me. "I've decided to step down as chairman. There's only one person I know who has the worldwide experience to take my place — and that's you. Think of it as another step in the call to unity. It would be the first time an organization that is strongly evangelical called a Roman Catholic to chair its board of directors."

I was thinking about people around the world who would be better qualified, and I started to beg off. "It's an international organization," I said. "Why don't you find a non-American?"

"We explored the possibility," he replied. "But the board agreed that it's still important we have an American as the chairman. We think you would be perfect for it."

I was extremely reluctant. "I don't know, Chuck. Nancy's paid such a huge price with me being gone, and she's asked me to cut back on activities." We were both looking forward to my governorship of Wayne State ending and the time that would free for us to spend together. But I promised Chuck I would pray about it.

Nancy and I started praying every night about the position. I didn't feel God's calling, but I didn't feel that I should turn down the offer either. As I've said, I had learned that God says "yes," "no," and "wait" in answer to our prayers. For some weeks, "wait" was the only answer I received.

Chuck kept calling and asking, "How are you doing? Any decision yet?"

"Chuck, I feel nothing."

"I can't believe you don't feel anything!" he said.

"Well, I don't," I responded. "And I'm not going to do it until the Lord gives me the go-ahead."

"I can't argue with that," he replied.

□ □ □

One night, I was lying in bed after Nancy and I'd prayed about the matter once more, and I began asking myself whether I was being fair to God in this decision. I decided that I'd take a few steps that might allow the Lord to speak to me more clearly.

I asked the president of Prison Fellowship International (PFI), Ron Nikkel, to our home for dinner. I wanted to see if he and I had the needed chemistry, since we would be working so closely together. At our dinner, Ron said something that greatly impressed me: "Going into prisons is often a difficult thing. I'm not in this because I love prisoners. I'm in this because Jesus loves prisoners."

That was profound, particularly coming from Ron, who is perhaps the most compassionate man I've ever met. He has spent the last twenty-five years going into prisons around the world and probably has ministered to more prisoners and prisoners' families than anyone in human history. Ron's job is much like an "area minister" in Protestant terms or a bishop in the Catholic world. He spends as much as 50 percent of his time on the road in what are usually uncomfortable circumstances, talking to PFI workers and the prisoners they work with, praying with them, giving guidance about confronting ministry and personal challenges. A man has to be truly Jesus' servant to do such work.

I asked Ron, "Why don't we take a trip together? That would be the litmus test for me." I knew that if we went into prisons together, I'd see how we might work as a team.

Ron is a strong, big-chested Canadian with russet-colored hair, a close-cropped beard, and a sunny, Huck Finn smile. He has the noble attribute of gravitas, a weight of character that derives from moral purpose. He's no one's fool. He bonds with people in whom he finds a similar integrity, which has brought a distinguished group of associates into PFI.

On our trip, we flew to Costa Rica and then on to Honduras. We worked well together in the prisons. In Honduras, we toured one prison with a volunteer who carried a medical kit. During the day, prisoners approached him with a variety of ailments, from gashes and wounds at risk of infection to flu-like symptoms.

Later than night, at dinner, I asked this volunteer if he was a doctor. In reply, he asked if I knew who Che Guevara was. Of course, I knew of this Marxist revolutionary who had helped bring Castro to power in Cuba. The volunteer told me he wasn't a doctor, but he had fought for years as a guerrilla alongside Che. From those years on the run, he had learned about basic medical care.

His life changed when he discovered that the true revolutionary was Jesus Christ. Now he was spending all his time, including daily prison visits, carrying out the revolution of Jesus' love. He had been threatened many times with death and warned to stop going into the prisons because he was destroying the drug trade behind prison walls. But he had found a cause that was truly worth his life. He would never stop.

My trip with Ron proved to be a turning point. I discovered him to be a man of unflagging patience and tremendous energy undergirded by his sense of calling. He took as much time with someone as that person needed, addressing the person's longing to be understood and cared for as well as specific problems. (This encourages me in my own lifelong battle with impatience.) At the same time, Ron abounds in energy—most people need to break into a jog to keep up with him in an airport.

□ □ □

When I arrived home from the trip, Nancy and I went to bed early. I was exhausted and struggling with jetlag. Before we went to sleep, we prayed together as we always do each night. Despite my fatigue, I sensed something different in her. "Did something happen while I was gone?" I asked.

"Yes," she answered.

"What?"

Nancy is the model of a level-headed person. What she said next stunned me. "God spoke to me," she said.

"Did you hear His voice?" I asked.

"A couple of times."

"Really?" I said. "More than once?"

She mentioned that our friend Roger, who is on the board at Cornerstone Schools, had sent her a book on George Mueller, the nineteenth-century evangelist who founded a number of orphanages in Bristol, England, that cared for thousands of children. Amazingly, Mueller never solicited funds for his orphanages or his other missionary endeavors; through his deep life of prayer, the needs of his ministries were always supplied.

"Did you know," Nancy asked, "that between the time he was seventy and ninety years old, Mueller traveled around the world several times? He journeyed more than two hundred thousand miles and preached to an estimated three million people."

"And, of course, that was long before air travel," I said, trying to imagine how I would handle sea voyages for months on end as an octogenarian.

"He went to the Middle East, North America, India, China, Australia, Japan—everywhere," Nancy continued. "Anyway, God told me you are like that. You are someone who's going to be traveling until the end of your life. You are going to keep talking about being a follower of Jesus. That's what God wants for you. And He wants me to support you in it."

This was not one of those moments when a husband wants to do something and his wife begrudgingly agrees. If anything, despite how well the trip had gone, I was still unsure of the call to the chairmanship of PFI. But Nancy's word from the Lord became my own as well. I knew I had to take the position.

I called Chuck the next day and told him what had happened—about the trip and Nancy's experience. I was installed as chairman the following November in Manila at a PFI council meeting. From that day until now, my service with PFI has been a continuation of what started through my trips with Doug. This work is far more hands-on than my previous efforts on behalf of The Fellowship, though. Not only do I meet with leaders on behalf of the poor, but I also meet with the people Chuck calls the "poorest of the poor" in what are truly the hellholes of the world, where I can boldly proclaim the gospel, which is the mission of PFI.

Meeting the poorest of the poor is the greatest privilege of my life. I meet prisoners who are so full of the Holy Spirit that it is humbling. Many times I feel like kneeling down in front of a prisoner and asking him to pray for me because I know he is so much holier than I am. Such prisoners have nothing but God, and that enables Jesus to be everything and to shine in their lives as He can with few others. When I see the presence of Jesus in a prisoner, my own faith increases. I realize that God's power is truly perfected in weakness, as St. Paul wrote. And I realize that God's grace is sufficient even for me.

□ □ □

Prison Fellowship International consists in a confederacy of indigenous ministries working in 114 countries. While much of the international office's support comes from America, each nation, even the poorest, supports its own ministry and contributes on a percentage basis to the international administrative costs. Collectively, the national ministries of PFI send more than one hundred thousand volunteers into prisons around the globe. That's an astounding figure—a miracle. It brings to mind Jesus' statement that by the power of the Holy Spirit His disciples will perform "greater works than these," His own miracles.

Prison Fellowship International is not merely another humanitarian program, but it defines itself as "a global volunteer-based *movement* working for the spiritual, moral, social, and physical well-being of prisoners, ex-prisoners, their families, crime victims, and criminal justice officials."

The practice of true ecumenism is at the heart of this worldwide movement. PFI President Ron Nikkel never tires of emphasizing the unity we have in Christ, as I try to do as well. All those involved with PFI unite as colleagues across the church's historical divisions and differences to lift up Jesus. We then reach out to the prisoner with God's offer of salvation; we do as much as we can to welcome their children into a loving community as well. We always keep in mind the need for justice and reparation for the victims of crime and the day-to-day hardships of guards and other corrections personnel.

Unlike any other ministry in the world today, PFI is truly ecumenical in that it is comprised of Protestant, Catholic, and Orthodox volunteers. The volunteers for a national PFI ministry usually come from a country's largest denominations. For example, in Latin America, most volunteers are Catholic and Pentecostal; in northern Europe, Protestant; in many parts of Eastern Europe, Greek or Russian Orthodox. PFI embraces the great heart of traditional faith, as found in the Apostles' and Nicene Creeds and in a statement of the mission's own that adds an emphasis on Scripture. PFI actually demands that no national ministry can be the captive of any particular denomination. That's how seriously we take our ecumenical stance.

I sometimes think that PFI's commitment to true ecumenism may be seen by historians as its most significant contribution. I hope and pray that history will see the ecumenism of PFI as a sign and a call that many other Christian endeavors heeded to the benefit of humankind. I know that what we are doing works. In country after country, PFI overcomes divisions within the church by joining together in our one Lord, Jesus Christ, because we combine ecumenism with evangelization. We don't proselytize—attempt to convert everyone to a single denomination—which is key to our success.

When I consider the strength we as Christians derive from unity, I think back to Pastor Max Lucado's appearances at Promise Keepers rallies. He would ask the huge crowds to shout out the names of the denominations to which they belonged. The calls of "Baptist," "Lutheran," "Methodist," "Presbyterian," "Greek Orthodox," "Assemblies of God," "Catholic," "Church of Christ," and so on produced a confused and unintelligible roar—a scattering of noise from another tower of Babel. But when Max asked who brought the men to the gathering, what was the name of their Savior, the men shouted out "Jesus! Jesus! Jesus!" His name sounded out over and over again, as strong, clear, and resonant as Gabriel's trumpet.

In Jesus' magnificent prayer to His Father, He asks, "that they may be brought to perfection as one, that the world may know that you sent me, and that you loved them even as you loved me" (John 17:23). For us to be in disunity is in direct defiance of Jesus' words and is in rebellion against this prayer and the exhortations of the New Testament. Sectarianism or denominationalism—whatever you wish to call it—is disunity. It is division. It is the seed of the Devil. We do not work for unity; we work to end and erase disunity. Unity is of God; disunity is of man.

In matters of doctrine and practice of conscience, our guide should be this traditional saying:

In essentials, unity.
In nonessentials, liberty.
But in all things, love.

What are the essentials of a believer? I believe they include the following:

- "God was reconciling the world to himself in Christ, not counting their trespasses against them and entrusting to us the message of reconciliation" (2 Corinthians 5:19).
- "Now this is eternal life, that they should know you, the only true God, and the one whom you sent, Jesus Christ" (John 17:3).
- "Amen, amen, I say to you, no one can see the kingdom of God without being born from above" (John 3:3).
- "For this is the will of my Father, that everyone who sees the Son and believes in him may have eternal life, and I shall raise him on the last day" (John 6:40).
- "At the name of Jesus every knee should bend, of those in heaven and on earth and under the earth, and every tongue confess that Jesus Christ is Lord, to the glory of God the Father" (Philippians 2:10-11).
- "If you confess with your mouth that Jesus is Lord and believe in your heart that God raised him from the dead, you will be saved. For one believes with the heart and so is justified, and one confesses with the mouth and so is saved" (Romans 10:9-10).

These are the essential truths that we who profess to believe in Jesus Christ must agree on. These are the holy words from God that He inspired to be written in the Bible. Most other teachings may be considered nonessentials, particularly in the context of doing ministry together as followers of Jesus. We need to reach out in love to a broken world, with the strong name of Jesus in our hearts and on our lips.

To work together on the basis of core Christian convictions across denominational and other divides remains difficult. What makes this possible within PFI is the wise application of that deeper sense of evangelism that I found in my own life as I matured as a believer. The staff and volunteers of PFI commit themselves to evangelizing themselves first, becoming ever more converted or sanctified in Christ's life. Only after we have found and stored up the love of Christ in ourselves and our coworkers do we seek to give that love away to the poorest of the poor. We can't give away what we do not possess ourselves.

Another distinguishing feature of PFI lies in its decentralized approach to new initiatives. The national ministries that make up PFI enter into a charter or membership agreement that licenses their affiliation. This agreement stipulates the organization's commitment to the historic Christian faith, to the vision and mission of PFI, and to working across the lines of Christian traditions and denominations. It does not, however, commit the ministry to adopting an American model of prison ministry, as if these ministries were so many McDonald's franchises. Rather, PFI provides training for a country's national leadership in working with chaplaincy programs, providing post-prison support, assisting children and families of prisoners, developing means of reconciling victims and offenders, and promoting the concept of restorative justice. PFI also makes available a host of instructional materials that have been found helpful elsewhere in conducting prison ministry. But each nation adapts what has been done elsewhere in terms of its own opportunities and needs.

PFI's decentralized approach has resulted in creative approaches springing up that Americans could not have envisioned. Most notably, the Association for Protection and Assistance to the Convicted (APAC) program, founded in São Paolo, Brazil, involves national prison ministries in running entire prisons or portions of prisons. APAC invites prisoners into a graduated program of spiritual formation and psychological and vocational development. Prisoners in Brazil, Ecuador, Grenada, and elsewhere progress from "spiritual boot camp" prison wings, where they receive intensive instruction and counseling, to more advanced residential settings or "homes." In these wings of the prison, offenders live together in circumstances that are so peaceful they remind visitors of religious communities.

While originating in Brazil, the APAC approach is now being tried in the United States, where it is called the InnerChange Freedom Initiative. Texas, Iowa, Kansas, Minnesota, and Arkansas already have programs up and running.[20]

In addition to the ground-breaking APAC program, PFI has seen such innovations as the Umuvumu Tree Project in Rwanda, which seeks reconciliation between victims and victimizers in the 1994 genocide. Jubilee Homes have begun in India, Nepal, and elsewhere for children effectively orphaned by their parents' incarceration. Other national ministries have begun running camps for the children of prisoners.

But the work of PFI can best be described through several individual cases that show its essential nature as a movement of the Holy Spirit. God calls what often seem the least likely people in the most difficult circumstances to do His work—the foolish of the world that He uses to confound the wise. To meet these men and women is one of the most inspiring experiences a person can have.

I think first of the Romanian Constantin Asavoaie, who grew up in a poor family with a violent, alcoholic father who died of his addiction when Constantin was only seven years old. Constantin became the "man of the family," pleading with the family's cow to provide enough milk for his mother and sisters.

Gifted with an extraordinary mind, Constantin made the highest score on a national exam used by the Communist Party to recruit future leaders. He became head of the Young Communists in Romania, determined to find a political means to address society's ills. This only led to despair, however, and as a young man Constantin tried to commit suicide, ingesting three hundred sleeping pills.

He took his survival as a sign that God had a purpose for his life and adopted his wife's Christian faith. He joined The Lord's Army, a renewal fellowship within Romania's Orthodox Church.

As a result of his conversion, Constantin soon fell out of favor with the Communist Party. The party used an accounting error in his office to send him to prison on embezzlement charges. He spent his time in prison developing his new life in Christ, devoting himself to prayer, fasting, and studying the Bible.

"I felt the strong work of the Holy Spirit," Constantin says of those days. In prison he read a copy of Colson's *Born Again*, which he soon translated so that the book could be published in Romanian. The work so inspired Constantin that he vowed to become the "Charles Colson of Romania."

Once released from prison, Constantin began ministering to those left behind, founding Prison Fellowship Romania in 1993. His depth of concern for prisoners also manifested itself in care for their families and those at risk of being drawn into a life of crime. Under Constantin's leadership, Prison Fellowship Romania has established three group homes: one for street children that includes many prisoners' children (protecting them from sexual traffickers and exploitation by other criminals); one for the homeless; and one for wives of the incarcerated and their children. More than five thousand staff and volunteers work in Prison Fellowship Romania programs throughout the country's thirty-seven prisons.

Beyond these concrete achievements, Constantin Asavoaie is known throughout Romania as a man of great integrity and an advocate for the poor. He helped established the first probation system in all of Eastern Europe. In 2003, he was named Romania's Man of the Year.

Once, after Constantin and I gave an interview together on Romanian television, a TV staffer said to me, "You know, your friend [Constantin] could be elected president of Romania if he were willing to run." I don't doubt it. But Constantin is committed to sacrificial living.

"I am personally so blessed," he says, "by working with wonderful young people full of vision and dreams."[21]

Then I think of those who minister in the Bellavista Prison in Medellin, Colombia. As anyone who has followed the wars among drug cartels in that country knows, Colombia has long been on the verge of collapsing into a culture of death. The epicenter of that culture was once Bellavista Prison. Most of the prisoners there were incarcerated for murders related to the drug wars. The various factions of Colombia's seditious culture — the paramilitary, guerrillas, corrupt military and police, leaders of the cartels and their mules — were all to be found in Bellavista, which made the prison the most violent in all of Latin America. Murders were a daily occurrence, with revenge being taken by the assassins of assassins.

The staff and volunteers of Prison Fellowship Colombia, chiefly made up of Catholics and Pentecostals, began to pray for Bellavista, led by a remarkable woman, Jeanine Brabon, a Methodist missionary who teaches in a seminary as well.

One day, a pastor and a group of men and women went up to a hill overlooking the prison. They prayed in earnest that somehow God's peace would come to Bellavista. One woman saw a vision of the prison in God's hand. The group took this as a sign that God would perform a miracle.

The worship of Bellavista's Church Behind Bars, with its congregation of five hundred, was piped out over the prison's loudspeaker system to seven thousand inmates. Gradually, it began to have amazing effects. Inmates ministered to their fellow inmates. A Bible institute began in the prison. The prisoners constructed a new chapel and a garden for meditation beside it. Prison Fellowship Colombia workers were able to institute a structured peace process that brought together many among the old factions and allowed them to find reconciliation. The cumulative effects of all these efforts have turned Bellavista, once the *most* violent prison in Latin America, into the *least* violent. Where God is, peace reigns.

Over twenty thousand people per week visit the prisoners of Bellavista. Families bring in aid to supplement the meager rations allowed by the prison itself. As the result of the interaction between the prisoners and the surrounding community, and the influence of the Church Behind Bars, thousands of conversions have taken place, the evangelistic efforts of the prison ministry rippling out into the community.

For example, Bellavista prisoner Jesus Amado Sarria was

watching TV when he saw his murdered wife being carried out of their home on the news. He was a major figure in Colombia's criminal world, working closely with drug cartel leader Pablo Escobar. During his imprisonment, Jesus became a follower of Jesus Christ and now regularly goes back into the prison to preach.

Not long ago, he met the man who murdered his wife. This man had become a believer as well. They were able to embrace as brothers in Christ. Jesus describes their reconciliation as a supremely painful moment. But he says the pain was separated from any form of hatred, revenge, anxiety, or anger. He imagines the pain the two men knew in their embrace as the pain Jesus suffered on the Cross for all of us.

Jeanine Brabon describes working at Bellavista Prison, using a local expression, as being "in the mouth of the lion." She says that the work advances on its knees in fasting and prayer, and she invites others to join her because "eternity will know the difference."

□ □ □

When I think of the work of PFI, I think finally of the condemned section in Uganda's Upper Prison, close to the capital city of Kampala. There Anglicans and other Protestants carry out much of PFI's work. The prison holds as many as twenty-five hundred men and looks like a big concrete box. In this concrete box is another concrete box, empty but for the 319 condemned men who live there.

There is not a stick of furniture inside the condemned section. The men sleep on the cement floor, and all they have are the rags on their backs and a blanket. While they have been condemned to death, the men do not know the dates of their executions.

Twenty-nine were once hanged on a single day. The rest await execution at the pleasure, so to speak, of the president. (I went to speak to him about this, and while I do not know the ultimate effect of my visit, no one has been executed since our conversation five years ago.)

Soon after the September 11 terrorist attacks in New York and Washington, I visited that condemned section. Every time I go into it, I see the Spirit of God at work. The condemned are excited about Christ, and they praise Him in a way as dramatic as I've ever seen or heard. Revival has come to the condemned.

When they receive visitors, the prisoners spread their prized blankets for us to sit on. Then they sing and praise God with all their hearts. While the concrete walls remain, they no longer seem impenetrable. Hearing the prisoners sing, I cannot doubt that once again the risen Lord has come through a locked door and stands in our midst.

On this occasion, after fifteen minutes of singing and prayer, the whole company sat down. Then the group's leader, Chris, one of the oldest men on death row, stood and addressed me. He began by calling me "Mizee," a term of respect that means "old one."

"Mizee," he said, "we want you to know that since September 11 we have been praying for the people of America."

I was shocked to hear him say this, because the terrorist attacks had taken place only a week before.

Chris went on. "We have been praying for the victims, for the families, and we would like you to take this message back to America: We, the condemned, stand with the people of America."

He asked his fellow prisoners to stand with him then and pray for the people of America.

"We are praying for wisdom for your president," he said. "We are standing with you before God."

These men were thinking of all Americans and especially their Christian brothers and sisters in America. Most of what they know personally of America comes by way of Christians who minister to them. So their hearts are with their fellow Christians.

When I've told people this story, I've been asked, "Mike, why would they care? Their lives are over. They have no hope in life. Why would they even think about us?"

"Because as true believers they understand something we don't," I've said. "That when one part of the body of Christ suffers, all of the body of Christ suffers."

If the "least of these," literally the condemned of the earth, can understand the unity of the body of Christ and reach out to those who suffer a world away, how can we do anything less for them? How can we allow the sin of disunity to prevent us from being united in the essentials so that we are channels of God's love to a suffering world? The unity of the body is a principle every Christian organization and follower of Jesus is called to embrace. It's essential to who we are as we find our lives hidden with Christ in God.

Looking Back, Looking Forward

As I look over my life, it's amazing to think what God has allowed me to see and do. The roles I've been called to play and the challenges entailed are continuing. Very often during the course of this writing, I marveled at how God continues to weave the threads shown here into an ever more elaborate pattern reflective of His glory. I've had to stop myself from saying, "That needs to go into the book, too. And that and that and that . . ." God's work is *the* never-ending story.

I've observed that the true mark of a follower of Jesus is that he or she never stops growing. When I consider the great men God has brought into my life, such as Cardinal Maida, the late Bill Bright, Doug Coe, and Chuck Colson; I see the God-centered passion and usefulness of these men only increases. That's my goal for how I want to live the rest of my life. I want to be more and more God's servant.

In my marriage, I have been blessed by a woman who has been willing to live her life with and for me. Nancy is just as committed to the cause of Christ as I am. She is a great adviser, comforter, and companion in all that God has called me to do.

I have been blessed as well with a son and daughter-in-law who are likewise committed to Christ. They are wonderful parents who have been called recently to demonstrate in a new way the sanctity of life. Our last grandchild, who is also named Michael, was born with a hole in his heart and with Down syndrome. His life will present unique challenges, but these will be borne through faith in Christ and the knowledge that baby Michael is made in the image and likeness of God. In God's eyes, Michael reflects His image as much as anyone. He will be loved and nurtured by his family. I expect to be taught many things about the goodness of God through his life.

In my business career, my partnership with my friend Randy Agley is finally coming to an end. We have contributed to the building of society through companies that manufacture useful goods and do so in innovative ways.

I've been so thrilled to see in Grosse Pointe and Detroit younger men and women embrace the cause of Christ. Through Bible studies, accountability groups, leadership retreats, and other means, the young Christian leaders of our community are reaching out to adults and children alike. This is truly a dream come true for Nancy and me. We're astounded at how much the Lord has prospered the faithful work of the "host couples." It takes only a handful of people to affect a broad community when they reach out in love and prayer in Christ.

At Prison Fellowship Ministry, we are going through a time of transition—one of the most difficult for any institution to accomplish—from a "personality-driven" ministry to a mission-centered ministry. This transition is being led with singular foresight by the "personality" that got it going, Chuck Colson.

There would have been no PF without Chuck's dynamic leadership. He is not only one of my closest friends but also a man who constantly encourages me like a big brother. No one has taught me more than Chuck about how the laity can network together for the good of the church. Clearly, he has done more for the unity of evangelicals and Catholics than any other evangelical leader and perhaps anyone period. I will never forget the role Chuck played in my installation as PFI chairman. In 1997, he stood before the crowd in Manila and pointed out the significance of the day. He as a Baptist and I as a Catholic were joining together as brothers in Christ for the least, the last, and the lost. When Chuck, along with other leaders, laid hands on me in a commissioning prayer, he helped bring about a new day in evangelical and Catholic relations. Before some evangelical supporters of the ministry saw me in action, they had their doubts. Many told me that his blessing of my role made a tremendous difference.

Chuck is leading the way once more, both through the transition going on at Prison Fellowship and in its commitment to ecumenism in the service of the gospel of Jesus Christ, both here and abroad. He's still teaching us how to reach out to "the least of these" and indeed to every member of society. He stepped down as chairman of PF USA in October 2006, to pursue his speaking, writing, and teaching to an even greater degree. For the good work of PF USA to continue long into the future, the ministry must become known more for the work it does than for its charismatic founder. No one knows this better than Chuck, who has been unusually wise in helping the ministry undertake this transition.

In October 2006, I assumed the chairmanship of both Prison Fellowship in the United States and PFI for what I hope will be a short period of three or four years. My role is to help Chuck and the trustees bring in new members capable of facing the next generation's challenges. That process is already well underway with the appointment five years ago of Mark Earley, the former attorney general of Virginia, as PF USA's president. Mark is a great leader and clearly God's man at this time. We are also engaged with an outstanding group of younger Christian leaders concerning future leadership roles.

As a Roman Catholic, I am particularly thrilled with the expansion of the men's movement throughout the United States. In the year this book is being published, approximately fifty events are planned to lift up Christ to Catholic men. I believe this is part of the realization of Vatican II's call to a "new evangelization." I see a hunger among Catholic men to know the Word of God—as Jesus said in Luke's gospel, "Put out into deep water" (5:4). Only in this way can we become the type of men and women God wants us to be.

For that to happen every person must, as Mother Teresa taught me, "totally surrender" to Christ. We have to be yielded to God. My continuing prayer is that I will find the grace to yield.

Notes

1. My dad's professional football career lasted seven years. He faced his brother across the line many times. Brian's contract was eventually sold to the Hamilton Tiger Cats, and he played and coached football for nineteen years. He was ultimately elected to the Canadian Football Hall of Fame.
2. Catholics' deep familiarity with many passages, on the other hand, can make Bible study especially exciting and rewarding for us; seeing how the familiar readings of the lectionary fit into the big picture can have a profound effect.
3. The renewal movement in the Catholic Church was encouraging Bible studies to spring up at this time in many dioceses, and a major center of the renewal existed not far away in Ann Arbor, but I had no knowledge of this.
4. Austin Flannery, OP, gen. ed., *Dei Verbum* in *Vatican Council II*, vol. 1 (Costello Publishing Company and Dominican Publications, 1998), 764.
5. Quotes in this paragraph are from *Dei Verbum*, 762–764.
6. Ralph Martin, *Hungry For God*, 15.
7. Martin, 19.
8. Martin, 20.
9. Martin, 35.

10. Father Michael Scanlan, *Let the Fire Fall*, 75.

11. Scanlan, 76.

12. As quoted in "Shields of Faith," *Envoy: Bringing Christ to the World*, http://www.envoymagazine.com/backissues/2.3/dip-lomaticcorps.html (accessed October 9, 2007).

13. As quoted in "Shields of Faith."

14. Fortunately, in 1992 the leader of the Shining Path, a former professor of philosophy named Abimael Guzmán, was captured, which led to the arrest and incarceration of virtually the entire leadership of the Shining Path. The violence in Peru quieted thereafter, although there remains much work to be done in the country.

15. *The Cloud of Unknowing*, chap. 35, par. 187. From the web at The Ethereal Library, Calvin College. The Middle English text reads as follows: "In this same course, God's word either written or spoken is likened to a mirror. Ghostly, the eyes of thy soul is thy reason; thy conscience is thy visage ghostly. And right as thou seest that if a foul spot be in thy bodily visage, the eyes of the same visage may not see that spot nor wit where it is, without a mirror or a teaching of another than itself; right so it is ghostly, without reading or hearing of God's word it is impossible to man's understanding that a soul that is blinded in custom of sin should see the foul spot in his conscience."

16. Congregation of Rites, *Eucharisticum mysterium*, 6, as found in *The Catechism of the Catholic Church*, 1325, 1334.

17. *Catechism*, 1332, 1336.

18. Even now there's a virtual civil war in the north of Uganda, led by Joseph Kony, who advocates a "theocracy," while kidnapping children and using them as human shields and sex slaves.

19. "A Perspective on Promise Keepers," by National Conference of Catholic Bishops' Committee on Marriage and Family, Bishop Joseph L. Charron, CPPS, Chairman, June 1996.

20. The Iowa program has become a test-case of faith-based initiatives as a suit against it has been brought by Barry Lynn and Americans United for Separation of Church and State. Prison Fellowship in the United States President Mark Earley predicts that the case will be decided finally by the Supreme Court.

21. "Former Romanian Prisoner Receives Humanitarian Award During National Prayer Breakfast Festivities," *Envoy Magazine*, http://www.wilberforce.org/article.asp?ID=196 (updated February 1, 2004).

About the Authors

MIKE TIMMIS was born in Detroit, Michigan, where he has had a distinguished career as both an attorney and businessman. He earned his undergraduate degree from Wayne State University and graduated with highest honors from the Wayne State Law School in 1965. He was an Editor of *Law Review* while in law school. He received the School's Distinguished Law Alumni Award in 1979. Mr. Timmis is a member of the Order of the Coif. Additionally, in 1991 Governor John Engler appointed him as a Governor of Wayne State University, the term of which expired December 31, 1996. In 1993, Mr. Timmis was the recipient of the Business and Professional Award from Religious Heritage of America. Further, Mr. Timmis received an Honorary Doctorate in Humane Letters degree from the University of Detroit-Mercy in May of 1995 in recognition of his civic and humanitarian contributions. In April, 1999, Mr. Timmis was the recipient of a Lifetime Achievement Award from William Tyndale College.

Mr. Timmis was senior partner of the law firm of Timmis & Inman L.L.P. He is also the cofounder and vice-chairman of Talon L.L.C., a privately owned company formed in 1973 with extensive interests in manufacturing and real estate companies.

In addition to his legal and business involvements, Mr. Timmis holds memberships in many professional associations; is a director of numerous corporations; and serves or has served in a leadership capacity on the boards of many charitable organizations and foundations, including St. John Healthcare Systems, Cornerstone Schools, Inc., The Navigators, and Wayne State University Foundation. Also, Mr. Timmis serves as Chairman of Prison Fellowship International comprising 112 chartered countries. In October 2006, Mr. Timmis succeeded Chuck Colson as Chairman of Prison Fellowship Ministries (USA) and, therefore, now co-chairs both Prison Fellowship entities.

Mr. Timmis and his wife, Nancy, are deeply involved in the problems of the poor in the Third World and have developed self-help projects in Africa and Central and South America. They are also active in addressing the educational needs of children in the City of Detroit. Along with his partner, Mr. Randolph Agley, Mr. Timmis was named one of the leaders of the Nineties by Crain's Detroit Business magazine.

Mr. Timmis is a Roman Catholic and a member of St. Paul Catholic Church, Grosse Pointe Farms, Michigan. He is also a member of the Knights of Malta and the Knights of the Holy Sepulchre, Legatus, is President of the Archdiocese of Detroit Endowment Foundation, Inc., is Trustee of the Pope John Paul II Cultural Center, and is one of the founding members of the National Fellowship of Catholic Men.

Mr. Timmis has been married to the former Nancy Lauppe for forty-five years. The Timmises have two children, a son Michael and a daughter Laura, who died twenty-two years ago. Their son and his wife (also named Laura) lived in Uganda, East Africa, for seven years lifting up Christ to the poor through various projects, which work continues in the five schools and in various programs for street children and the rural poor in Uganda and Rwanda. Currently, Michael Timmis Jr. serves as President of the Timmis Family Foundation. The junior Timmises are graduates of University of Michigan receiving MBA's from the School of Business. The junior Timmises live in Florida and have three daughters and one son. The senior Timmis family resides in Grosse Pointe Farms, Michigan, and Naples, Florida.

HAROLD FICKETT is author of *The Holy Fool*, *Flannery O'Connor: Images of Grace*, *The Living Christ*, and other books. He is cofounder of the journal *Image* and associate editor of the online social network *God Spy* (www.godspy.com). Charles Colson and he have recently completed *The Faith* (March, 2008).

Check out these titles from NavPress Deliberate.

The God Who Smokes
Timothy Stoner

ISBN-13: 978-1-60006-247-6
ISBN-10: 1-60006-247-4

Perhaps no recent spiritual movement has caused more division than the emergent church. For some, the trend represents a refreshing resistance to fundamentalist attitudes. For others, the ideas suffer from a lack of sound theology. Is there a middle ground? With a casual, narrative voice, Timothy Stoner presents an honest look at a controversial subject.

Free to Be Bound
Jonathan Wilson-Hartgrove

ISBN-13: 978-1-60006-190-5
ISBN-10: 1-60006-190-7

Jonathan was a product of the new South: color-blind and culturally sensitive. Yet despite his progressive worldview, he was unaware of the invisible borders separating neighborhood churches. *Free to Be Bound* chronicles Jonathan's experience as he crosses color lines that fragment the church. With an honest heart and passionate voice, he deliverers a call for true unity within the church that will inspire every believer.

The End of Religion
Bruxy Cavey

ISBN-13: 978-1-60006-067-0
ISBN-10: 1-60006-067-6

In *The End of Religion*, Bruxy Cavey contends that the Jesus described in the Bible never intended to found a new religion; instead he hoped to break down the very idea of religion as a way to God. With a fresh perspective on biblical stories, Cavey paints a picture of the world God originally intended and still desires: a world without religion.

To order copies, visit your local Christian bookstore, call NavPress at
1-800-366-7788, or log on to www.navpress.com.
To locate a Christian bookstore near you, call 1-800-991-7747.